MORE THAN LORE

ALMA MATER

THE UNIVERSITY SONG OF
THE UNIVERSITY OF CHICAGO

Today we gladly sing the praise
    Of her who owns us as her sons;
Our loyal voices let us raise,
    And bless her with our benisons.
Of all fair mothers, fairest she,
    Most wise of all that wisest be,
Most true of all the true, say we,
    Is our dear Alma Mater.

Her mighty learning we would tell,
    Tho' life is something more than lore;
She could not love her sons so well,
    Loved she not truth and honor more.
We praise her breadth of charity,
    Her faith that truth shall make men free
That right shall live eternally,
    We praise our Alma Mater.

The City White hath fled the earth,
    But where the azure waters lie,
A nobler city hath its birth,
    The City Gray that ne'er shall die.
For decades and for centuries,
    Its battlemented towers shall rise,
Beneath the hope-filled western skies,
    'Tis our dear Alma Mater.

MORE
THAN LORE

REMINISCENCES OF
MARION TALBOT

Dean of Women
The University of Chicago
1892–1925

With a Foreword by
HANNA HOLBORN GRAY

The University of Chicago Press ✳ *Chicago and London*

The University of Chicago Press, Chicago 60637
The University of Chicago Press, Ltd., London
© 1936 by The University of Chicago
Foreword © 2015 by The University of Chicago
All rights reserved. Published 2015.

Printed in the United States of America

24 23 22 21 20 19 18 17 16 15   1 2 3 4 5

ISBN-13: 978-0-226-31670-3 (cloth)
ISBN-13: 978-0-226-34679-3 (e-book)

Library of Congress Cataloging-in-Publication
Control Number: 2015026234

♾This paper meets the requirements of ANSI/NISO Z39.48-1992
(Permanence of Paper).

Contents

Foreword

Marion Talbot's *More than Lore* is neither an autobiography, although it contains elements of one, nor a full-scale memoir. It is her account, composed more than a decade after her retirement, of the beginnings and growth of a university to which she was warmly devoted, of its founding ambitions and their evolution, and of its contributions to the cause of higher education with special attention to that of women's education in a coeducational environment. Talbot's reminiscences concentrate on several major themes: the nature, and the excitements, of the University's earliest days; the development of a residential house system; the issues of women's place, both as students and as faculty, over changing times; and the creation of a new department in the field that came to be called home economics. Above all, she is concerned with the question of what equality in higher education should mean for women.

Drawn to the new university in large part by its charter's words of commitment "to provide, impart, and furnish opportunities for all departments of higher education to persons of both sexes on equal terms," Talbot worked hard to see that the university made good on this promise. She chronicled its successes but also, with a critical (yet still tactful) tone, the shortcomings she encountered, both at Chicago and in the wider universe of higher education, in realizing more fully the aims of genuine equality for women. She participated in the debates of her time over what the charter's phrase could and should really mean for women then and in the future.

The University of Chicago was not the first or even the first private coeducational university, and its opening coincided closely with that of Stanford (1891). Marion Talbot had attended Boston University (chartered in 1869) for both a bachelor's and a master's degree. BU was the only coeducational institution in Massachusetts. Coeducation had taken hold in some liberal arts colleges well before 1890: for example, Oberlin, Grinnell, Antioch, and Carleton in the Midwest; Swarthmore and Middlebury in the East; and, finally, Occidental and Pomona in the Far West. And coeducation was the norm also at many public universities including Wisconsin (1867) and Michigan (1870). Cornell, at once public and private, reluctantly admitted women in the early 1870s.

In most of these universities, there was and still remained considerable opposition to women's entrance, and there were frequent attempts to forestall this outcome and to create separate women's colleges within or affiliated with the universities. But fiscal realities and considerations, as well as legal concerns and the persistence of individual women who were determined to strive for advanced education, had turned the tide.[1] Still, some of that resistance continued to mark the outlook of many faculty, students, and boards, and the early twentieth century saw a resurgence of opposition to, and of attempts to reverse, coeducation where it existed. This movement reflected a profound fear that institutions, and the men who attended them, would be overwhelmed by the encroaching numbers of women students. Out of this concern and a mounting anxiety expressed over the "feminization" of higher education, there emerged a renewed call for the "segregation of the sexes" in undergraduate programs. Dean Talbot fought tenaciously against this at Chicago, and the battle is one of her prominent themes. Chicago was not alone in looking to separate undergraduate classes, but certainly, in her view, Chicago should be *better*.

A number of private universities had side-stepped coeducation by contracting with women's colleges as their affiliates; the Harvard Annex (later Radcliffe College), Pembroke at Brown, Barnard at Columbia, Jackson at Tufts, and Sophie Newcomb at Tulane are examples. But the largest innovation in women's education arose with the establishment of separate women's colleges, including those eastern colleges, all founded before 1890, that came to be called the Seven Sisters.

The period between 1870 and 1890, which included Marion Talbot's formative years and early career, witnessed a boom in American higher education. In 1870, fewer than 30 percent of colleges and universities admitted women; by 1890, the figure had grown to 43 percent (and by 1910, to 58 percent.) Enrollments of women in higher education grew in that time from around 11,000 to 56,000, with an enormous escalation to follow (85,000 in 1900; 140,000 in 1910), increases that exceeded the rate of growth for men. By 1890, fewer than 1,000 PhD degrees had been awarded in America; of those, women had earned a mere 3 percent. Only one woman had received a PhD before 1880; 24 in the decade of the '80s. The number rose eightfold in the 1890s, while that of men increased threefold, and the University of Chicago had trained more women with doctorates than had any other institution of the decade. After the turn of the century the higher education boom persisted at a rapid pace.[2]

What persisted also were questions having to do with the rationale for higher education for women. In the 1870s and '80s, the views expressed with special force and an air of medical authority by one Dr. Edward Clarke were widely circulated, often taken seriously, and ultimately hotly debated by those of other views. His investigations, set out at greatest length in his publications of 1873 and 1874, *Sex Education, or a Fair Chance for the Girls* and *Building a Brain*, concluded that women's health and capacity to bear children would be fatally affected were they to take up collegiate studies (in particular, because excessive study diverted blood from the ovaries to the brain).[3] Marion Talbot was well aware of these judgments and vigorously helped refute them, quoting with relish Dr. Clarke's prose: "The identical education of the two sexes is a crime before God and humanity that physiology protests against and that experience weeps over." By 1890 women who pursued higher education had successfully countered Dr. Clarke by their actions, but there lingered in the air some belief that women's health might indeed be at risk. The larger question, however, for Talbot and her contemporaries, became that of defining an "identical education," given the disparities seen or asserted as existing between men and women.

It is against this backdrop that one may best understand Talbot's career and its accomplishments.

Talbot was something of a pioneer even before her decision to go to Chicago.[4] Under the conditions of restricted schooling for girls, and with the support of her progressive parents, she had managed to get into Boston University and to earn two degrees; she had also received a bachelor of science degree from MIT, studying with Ellen Richards. Richards was one mentor; Alice Freeman Palmer, who as president of Wellesley College brought Talbot there as an instructor and as a protégé, another.

Ellen Richards, the first woman graduate student at MIT and the first woman to receive a PhD in chemistry, was regarded as the founder of "sanitary science." It represented a combination of studies that included economics, biology, chemistry, and public health (Talbot later added sociology, government, anthropology, and law) that was ultimately to become the field of home economics. Talbot predicted to University of Chicago president William Rainey Harper that home economics would come to be "given a place among the new social sciences as honorable as that which Political Economy or the Science of Government occupies."[5]

Alice Freeman Palmer was a distinguished and well-known figure whose presidency of Wellesley College and subsequent activities on behalf of higher education gave her a high national profile. She helped shape the standards perceived as those of the women's colleges: high academic aspirations for students and faculty together with a residential community in which the social training of undergraduates took place to produce educated, public-spirited, and well-rounded young women ready to deal with the world.[6] In the not even thinly disguised novel *Chimes*, written by Robert Herrick, an early and unhappy member of the University of Chicago's English department, Mrs. Palmer appears as Mrs. Crandall, sympathetically portrayed as elegant, intelligent, sensitive, tasteful, and humane (a counter to the materialistic, commercially minded, power-hungry, and somewhat vulgar, if successful, President Harris) who exercised a wide and beneficial influence on both administration and faculty and who gave a certain tone to both the university and the unpleasant, hucksterish, uncultivated city of Chicago, a tone sadly missed after her departure. Herrick called Mrs. Crandall's successor as dean of women "Gertrude Porridge," describing her as "an austere, remote individual." Whether this was meant to portray Dean Talbot, and whether she was so regarded by others, is unclear. Dean Porridge never reappears in the novel.[7] By contrast, the dean who emerges from the pages of *More than Lore* certainly seems to have a quiet charm and a sense of humor together with a taste for (virtuous) pleasure. She also conveys a different, very positive perspective on both the university and the city. In Chicago, she found a city that she considered to be transforming itself into a cultural and intellectual center.

The young Talbot was convinced that a new age was dawning for women's lives and responsibilities. In her writings she stressed how the changes that had taken place—the services and products that had replaced the need for women to produce everything from bread to clothing in the home and the technologies that had streamlined and rendered more efficient the running of a household, such as the electric stove and the telephone—had made it possible and necessary to prepare women for their lives through a broad higher education. Women would now be able to take up professions outside the home even beyond those of teaching and nursing, and household management itself could now be understood and developed as a science with academic status and scholarly weight.[8]

But when she graduated from Boston University in 1880, Talbot found herself seeing no clear occupation or future. As Ellen Fitzpatrick has observed, "The great contradiction of the revolution in women's higher education was that it prepared the first college graduates for a world of opportunities that did not really exist."[9] At the same time, Talbot felt totally isolated from her own contemporaries who were leading conventional and home-focused lives that no longer attracted her. With her mother's encouragement, she became a founder and the secretary of a new organization, the American Collegiate Association (later, in 1921, renamed the American Association of University Women). Bringing together women graduates of many different institutions who could befriend and support one another and be advocates for women's education became both a useful occupation and a cause. Talbot recounts the formation of this organization and her role in its affairs in these pages. The ACA took raising funds for women's graduate fellowships as a special goal, as the AAUW has done ever since, and she wanted very much to see women advance into the academic ranks of college and university faculties.[10] It is significant that, all her life, she brought together and constituted unified and purposeful groups and associations and clubs to carry forward her ideals. This strategy is reflected in her accounts of setting up women's organizations at the University of Chicago.

Given the spread of coeducation despite often fierce opposition, Talbot found much that was innovative and appealing in the plan for the University of Chicago. The pledge to pursue equality for its students was, she thought, only one aspect of its innovative undertaking. Other aspects had to do both with the university's emphasis on graduate study and its provision of fellowships for women from the start and with the fact that there were to be women on its first faculty. Finally, Mrs. Alice Freeman Palmer's urgings to accompany her on the great adventure of the new university in the "wild and woolly" city of Chicago were hard to reject. Mrs. Palmer and her husband were both offered appointments by President Harper—an early and rare instance of a couple being recruited to an academic institution—but Mr. Palmer could not be lured away from Harvard. Hence the arrangements Mrs. Palmer made to be in residence at Chicago for only three months of the year and her need for a loyal and competent assistant. Hence, too, the quite important role that Marion Talbot might play from the moment of her arrival.

Talbot does not discuss here the proposal she initially made to Harper that her appointment be at the level of associate rather than assistant professor or that she be made head of a department of public health (i.e., sanitary science). But she gives no sign in these pages that she was dissatisfied; on the contrary, as she first becomes acquainted with Harper, she writes about him admiringly and affectionately and with a little amusement as well. Like many others, she felt he was an utterly overwhelming force of nature endowed with extraordinary vision, persuasive power, and vitality. Her vivid description of her arrival in Chicago, the excitements of residence at the Hotel Beatrice, of a muddy unfinished campus, and the first faculty meeting, show her swept away by Harper's strength and personality. Moreover, her expectations of the new university appeared confirmed by the numbers of women undergraduates, graduate fellows, and faculty who were present at the start. She felt sure that early demonstrations of boorish misbehavior—for example, she describes a major reception given by the trustees for the members of the university that ended with the disappearance of the forks and spoons and table decorations—could be moderated. And she describes an athletic scandal—yes, they were born at once with the institution of intercollegiate sports—and commended Amos Alonzo Stagg for his response.

Mrs. Palmer's mandate turned out to be a broad one, and her influence in the first few years of the university's existence out of proportion to the time she spent there. Asked to take on the role of a dean of women, she became a close and important all-purpose counselor to the president, advising on faculty appointments and other policy matters. She was active in fundraising and became close to a number of Chicago's leading (and wealthy) women, including trustee wives, welcoming them into a lasting and productive association with the university. All this added to her central accomplishment, in partnership with Talbot, of planning and bringing into being the residential house system for women. Talbot and Palmer agreed on "liberty, equality, unity, and social responsibility" as the appropriate values and goals for the university's women students and their social mores. Instituting these priorities meant not imposing detailed and rigid rules but instead fostering self-government and personal independence in the houses, trying to prevent the emergence of sororities and secret societies, nurturing a sense of community, and encouraging cooperation and service through the conduct and activities of the students in their residential houses. Both women thought a certain degree of refinement, taste, and comfort essential in these surroundings; both wanted to guide their charges to proper decorum (Talbot makes quite evident what that entailed in writing about it at length in these pages); both thought a degree of flexibility and allowance for enjoyment and genuine pleasure should be welcomed as a rebuttal against the puritanical views of fundamentalists who disapproved of drinking and dancing for young women, let alone their consorting freely with men. Both were clear that the overriding priority of the university and of student life should be academics. In some ways, Palmer and Talbot adapted the models and standards of the eastern women's colleges to the coeducational environment of Chicago—not surprising, given Mrs. Palmer's career at Wellesley and Talbot's time there.[11]

It was Talbot who over time enunciated and oversaw the policies that embodied these principles. The hopes of the two women to create a women's center with every amenity was to culminate in Talbot's oversight of the construction and furnishing of Ida Noyes Hall. With Mrs. Palmer's departure from the university, Talbot became first, in 1895, dean of women in the graduate schools (and associate professor as well) and then, in 1899, Dean of Women, a title that, she claimed, the university was first to use. After her retirement, the university never had another Dean of Women.

In her academic role, Talbot was first assigned to the Department of Social Science, later to become Sociology, where she found herself kindly welcomed by Albion Small. The department was, so to speak, interdisciplinary before the individual disciplines broke out to form departments of their own, and Talbot's teaching of sanitary science could initially be housed under its umbrella, even if her program existed as an island of its own.[12] But Talbot never gave up her dream of a new department for her specialized subject that was itself conceived as interdisciplinary. In 1904, her wish was finally granted, under the name of Household Management, later to become Home Economics. The department, Talbot thought proudly, proved the continuing capacity for innovation and leadership in new fields and approaches to learning that had always characterized the University of Chicago.

President Harper may have given way finally in part as an act of atonement for having sought, in almost a panic over an inundation of female enrollments, to create a women's quadrangle with every facility that men possessed in theirs and to hold separate classes for men and women at least in the Junior College (the first two years of the College). His proposed policy was strenuously opposed by Talbot, by many alumnae, and by some, but not too many, faculty members, including John Dewey. The opposition lost, but the new rules were not made compulsory, and the whole effort quickly petered out on its own, to Talbot's great delight. She tweaks Harper over these events in the chapter "King of France," while also making clear her deep outrage that such a plan could ever have been thought of.

The battle over the segregation of the sexes was, however, a turning point in the history of coeducation and how it was practiced at the university, and this at a time when the same issues were being debated elsewhere.[13] Talbot saw that Harper was perhaps not so solid on the principle of equality for women and needed regular nudging on the issue. She had been arguing energetically that women were not only academically equal to men but were performing as well or better. In addition, they were choosing to study subjects, such as the sciences, that were usually thought more popular and relevant for men. Her annual reports made this case over and over, tabulating and analyzing the accomplishments as well as the numbers of the very successful women students for whom she was an advocate. At the same time, and ironically, the founding of the Department of Household Management did in fact create an academic space that, despite claims to represent a new social science analogous to others, constituted a course of study essentially for women. It presupposed a central role for women in the home even as Talbot was insisting on the professional careers for which women had the right, and now the educational opportunities, to be educated. It became an academic home to which women might be relegated and a subject less valued in terms of academic weight than were the major social sciences. It might be (and it has been) interpreted as a kind of segregation. In 1911 it was estimated that 60 percent of women faculty in coeducational institutions were teachers of home economics, many with their graduate degrees from Chicago. Talbot's department had opened a new area for aspiring academic women, one in which they could find employment. At the university in 1929, 1,150 students were registered in the

Home Economics Department. Twenty years later the number
was down to 45, and the department was finally closed in 1956.[14]

In her depiction of the first decade after the beginnings, a
darker, less optimistic note begins to enter Talbot's view of the
university and of the women's educational movement of her era.
She describes a growing difficulty in finding agreement on just
the right balance between women's special character and needs
as met in the university's social and residential system on the one
hand and the goals of educating women with full respect both
for their equal status and for their inevitably gendered role in the
larger world on the other. The university was proud of its record
in training PhDs, but in general women with doctorates were not
finding appointments at coeducational universities and colleges.
An AAUP report of 1921 found that at these institutions, 1,600
out of 13,000 were women, and that these women lagged in com-
pensation, promotion, and faculty status. They were quite likely
to be teaching education, nursing, or home economics. Women
PhDs found academic positions principally at the women's colleges where they could be a majority.

By the end of the university's first decade, Talbot observed
very little growth in number of women faculty while male faculty rapidly increased in number, a perceptible slowness in the
promotion of women, and a slowdown in fellowship offerings
for female graduate students as well as disparities of compensa-
tion between men and women. She believed that although the
university had done and was continuing to do better than others, it was not enough, and she voiced her disappointment. In
1924, and on the eve of retirement, Talbot launched an appeal,
joined by Edith Foster Flint and Elizabeth Wallace, to the board
of trustees to undertake a fresh effort to secure equality for wom-
en at the university. Her chapter "The Weaker Sex" summarizes
the record of women's achievement while deploring the relative
lack of continuing progress that followed in the decades after the

promise so boldly held out at the university's opening, pointing out that, in addition to those inadequacies, there had never yet been a woman trustee.

As Talbot grew older, she saw the university's beginnings more and more as a golden age full of adventure and unity and hope but the nearer present, especially after what she believed a negative and revolutionary change in social customs after the First World War, as failing fully to make good on those early accomplishments. But she never lost her conviction that the University of Chicago had done things, and represented a level of quality and of innovation, far beyond what any other institution of higher education had achieved, that it had indeed led the way for others in many respects. She believed firmly that it could still do so. Even at the end of "The Weaker Sex," she opposes the counsels of gloom and asserts better possibilities to come.

In a letter of 1940 to Robert Maynard Hutchins, a more elderly Marion Talbot was not, perhaps, so sure. Complaining about the flighty girls now at college, she wrote: "Responsibility and intelligence were indeed the keynotes one struck in those pioneering days and maintained for a number of years. Unfortunately the women have recently been 'slipping' due in considerable measure to the pernicious influence of the Maroon which has been clearly felt in many ways, in part also to their ageold [sic] subjection to habit and social standards."[15]

But perhaps she was just having a bad day.

Marion Talbot and her colleagues were among those who set a legacy within the university that still resonates in its residential system and in the coeducational goals that she so much wanted to see strengthened and fulfilled. (She would probably have been shocked, however, to find coeducational dormitories.) Talbot would have been gratified that her university was the first of its kind to appoint a woman president, but she would have asked, immediately and sharply, about how things looked at the heart of the university: its record of faculty appointments and of equal opportunities for women to benefit from all the university's resources. She would have been most concerned with the state of the dilemma that constantly preoccupied her and her colleagues and that has never died down even while taking new forms over the succeeding generations and eras: how to balance equality with gender difference and, in the end, what that should mean for scholarship, for learning, and for the structures of higher education.

HANNA HOLBORN GRAY

Harry Pratt Judson Distinguished Service Professor Emerita of History,
University of Chicago President, University of Chicago, 1978–1993

Notes

1. See Barbara Miller Solomon, *In the Company of Educated Women* (New Haven: Yale University Press, 1985), 53, for the long list of coeducational universities in existence before 1890. A holdout was the University of Virginia, which waited until 1970 to admit women.

2. For growth and enrollment figures, see Solomon, *Educated Women*, 44, 58; Ellen F. Fitzpatrick, *Endless Crusade: Women Social Scientists and Progressive Reform* (New York: Oxford University Press, 1994), 73–75, and Rosalind Rosenberg, *Beyond Separate Spheres: Intellectual Roots of Modern Feminism* (New Haven: Yale University Press, 1982), 32 n. 10.

3. See Rosenberg, *Beyond Separate Spheres*, 12–17, and Solomon, *Educated Women*, 56–71.

4. For Talbot's biography, her own papers in the Special Collections of the Joseph Regenstein Library of the University of Chicago are the best source. Aspects of her biography, at least in summary form, can be found in the following works cited elsewhere: Borodin, *Alice Freeman Palmer;* Fitzpatrick, *Endless Crusade* and "For the 'Women of the University'"; Gordon, *Gender and Higher Education;* Rosenberg, *Beyond Separate Spheres;* and Solomon, *Educated Women.*

5. Quoted in Solomon, *Educated Women*, 85. See also Ellen F. Fitzpatrick, "For the 'Women of the University,'" in *Lone Voyagers: Academic Women in Coeducational Universities 1870–1937*, ed. Geraldine J. Clifford (New York: Feminist Press at the City University of New York, 1989), 89.

6. On Palmer, see Ruth Bordin, *Alice Freeman Palmer: The Evolution of a New Woman* (Ann Arbor: University of Michigan Press, 1993).

7. Robert Herrick, *Chimes* (New York: Macmillan, 1926), 92.

8. For Talbot's views on women's education for a new world and for her work on sanitary science, see her major published books: *The Education of Women* (Chicago: University of Chicago Press, 1910); *Household Sanitation: Manual for Housekeepers* (Boston: Whitcomb & Barrows, 1919); and, with Sophonisba Breckenridge, *The Modern Household* (Boston: Whitcomb & Barrows, 1910 and subsequent editions through 1919). Talbot's annual reports on "The Women of the University" include extensive facts and figures on students and faculty as well as her descriptions of women's achievements in academic and extracurricular affairs. See, as a prime example at the time of the conflict over "segregated" education at the University, her report in the *Decennial Publications of the University of Chicago*, ser. I, vol. 1 (Chicago: University of Chicago Press, 1903). Her sense of the difficulties faced by female graduates in their relations with family expectations is summarized in her essay, "The College, the Girl, and the Parents," in *North American Review*, September 1910, 349–58.

9. Fitzpatrick, *Endless Crusade*, 8.

10. See Marion Talbot and Lois Rosenberry, *The History of the American Association of University Women, 1881–1931* (Boston: Houghton Mifflin, 1931).

11. See Bordin, *Alice Freeman Palmer*, 232–59, and Gordon, *Gender and Higher Education*, 92–102.

12. On Talbot's position in the department and her relations with the sociologists, see Mary Jo Deegan, *Jane Addams and the Men of the Chicago School, 1892–1918* (New Brunswick, NJ: Transaction Books, 1986), 192–96.

13. See especially Gordon, *Gender and Higher Education*, 112–17, and Solomon, *Educated Women*, 58–60, as well as *On Equal Terms: Educating Women at the University of Chicago*, ed. Monica Mercado and Katherine Turk (Chicago: University of Chicago Library, 2009), 17.

14. *On Equal Terms* (no page no.) On Talbot's department, the spread of Home Economics, and Chicago's role in training PhDs, see especially Fitzpatrick, *Endless Crusade*, 85–86; Gordon, *Gender and Higher Education*, 99–101; Rosenberg, *Beyond Separate Spheres*, 99–100; and Solomon, *Educated Women*, 85–87.

15. Marion Talbot to Robert Maynard Hutchins, June 8, 1940. This letter is reprinted in Fitzpatrick, "For the 'Women of the University,'" 123–24; the quotation is from 123.

Preface

Huge blocks of stone, steel girders, roofs of tile, have gone to make the "city gray that ne'er shall die"; but that is not all. Mortar and plaster and wood—lighter and seemingly less durable materials—are needed to make the stouter stuffs fit for human use. Architect and draftsman, financier and administrator, mechanic and artisan, have put their labor into it.

So it is with the life and labor which have gone on in it. Great libraries and laboratories have yielded up their treasures to the scholars whose researches made the University in a few short years world-renowned. On the other hand, personal contacts and social experiences—seemingly slight and unimportant matters—have served to make the community of scholars, old and young, a living reality. Problems of human living have had to be solved. It is with this in mind that the following memories of the past have been written. They are intended to supplement the ponderous and accurate records of the major achievements of the University and to show that it has been just "folks" who have built their daily living, as well as their ideals and their faith, into the institution which has proved to be one of the country's greatest achievements.

MORE THAN LORE

The Trek

Life will always be full of adventures as long as human perspectives change with age and values vary with experience. It was certainly very exciting to have Santa Claus write me a real letter and tell me that he was sending me a new doll and that I must be more careful and not smash its china head, as I did my dear old dolly's head. Another great adventure into a rich field was the Christmas gift of a set of the Rollo books, twelve in number, bound in green and gold and packed in a box, the most sumptuous Christmas gift I ever had, not excelled even by the Davenport desk which was my birthday present when I was ten years old. And life went on, and year after year brought thrilling experiences. One might perhaps become blasé, as it is said the present generation early becomes. But no lapse of years or train of interesting happenings in travel, education, or social life could deaden the sense of adventure when the call came to help organize the new University of Chicago. Stories of the new educational venture in the West had reached Boston. Its novel features— such, for example, as unprecedentedly large salaries, continuous instruction throughout the year, the organization of Extension Work, a Press, University Affiliations, Junior and Senior Colleges, and many others—gave rise to ridicule and sarcastic comment; but underneath, the educational world felt very real interest in the venture.

The gifted young president, William Rainey Harper, scoured the academic world for great scholars who would dare exchange

President W. R. Harper

comfortable and safe positions for the hazards and excitements of a new undertaking. Among those whom he most strongly urged were George Herbert Palmer, of Harvard University, to be head of the new Department of Philosophy, and his wife, Alice Freeman Palmer, formerly president of Wellesley College and at the time in the forefront of the chief educational movements in Massachusetts, to be professor of history and dean (of women) in the Graduate School and College. For a long time Professor and Mrs.

Palmer were unable to reach a decision, swayed, as they were, on the one side by the many opportunities and inducements offered, and, on the other, by the strength of long-established ties and enterprises already undertaken. Mrs. Palmer and I had worked in close and intimate accord in the Association of Collegiate Alumnae, which had been founded ten years previously and in which she maintained an active part to the end of her life. This experience began the year after I received my Bachelor's degree from Boston University. As secretary for a long period, I had an unusual opportunity to study collegiate and university conditions in the United States. This experience was supplemented with study which led to the Master's degree at Boston University and a more specialized degree in science at the Massachusetts Institute of Technology, with the secretaryship and later the presidency of the Massachusetts Society for the University Education of Women, with membership on the Board of Visitors of Wellesley College and later an instructorship at the same college, and with a term of service as alumni trustee of Boston University.

In April, 1892, Professor and Mrs. Palmer visited Chicago and met with much encouragement from influential men and women. Still in doubt, Mrs. Palmer wrote me, "Remember, if I come West you must come too—I mean it, my dear friend." Later on, in July, when the arrangement was made by which Mrs. Palmer would take an active share in the administration and be in residence at the University during twelve weeks of each year, she wrote me again, "I made my going conditioned on yours. Dr. Harper says that he distinctly wants you and will try to get you to Chicago for the start." When finally, in the late summer of 1892, the appointment came to be assistant professor of sanitary science and dean (of women) in the University Colleges, I had mingled feelings of interest and hesitation. The work at Wellesley in domestic science which I had started was full of promise. The secretaryship of the Association of Collegiate Alumnae brought important duties. My home ties were becoming increasingly close, and my circle

Marion Talbot, 1892

of friends was large. My mother, however, had taken joy in training her children for service according to their several gifts. Moreover, she had been in Chicago—a rather unusual experience in
those days for a Bostonian—and had been greatly impressed
with its spirit. She was convinced that I should cast in my lot
with the new University and the growing city. So, though it cost
her many a heart pang, she encouraged me to accept. My father
also, to whom I was giving clerical assistance in his medical and
philanthropic work, set aside his wish to keep me near him and
set his mind on the opportunities the future would bring to me.
Chicago seemed a very wild and woolly place to my friends, and
they were almost horrified at the idea of my leaving Boston, even
though some of them had a glimmer of an idea of the honor and
responsibility involved. Many of them expressed the hope that I
would soon return, and some were quite certain that I would get
enough of the West pretty soon. But preparations went on for my
departure. There were clothes to be bought, suitable for many
kinds of occasions and enough to last several months, and even
seasons, for there would be no time or strength for shopping or
dressmakers. The outfit seemed almost like a modest trousseau.
To add to the impression that I was about to change my state, not
only Massachusetts for Illinois, but spinsterhood for matrimony,
kind and thoughtful friends provided me with silverware, attractive dishes and bric-a-brac, and even linen.

At last came the time for departure. Mrs. Palmer and Mr.
William Gardner Hale were to be my traveling companions, and
quite a crowd of friends assembled at the station in Boston to see
us off on September 19, 1892. Florence M. Cushing, an honored
graduate of Vassar College with whom I had done educational
work for several years, pressed into my hand a small carved box.
In gentle and rather solemn tones she said, "It contains a piece
of Plymouth Rock." I felt the gift was rather symbolical of the attitude of Boston educators to the new undertaking. Those were
shifting and perilous sands out there on the edge of the prairie, as

it seemed to the dwellers on Beacon Hill. I must be reminded that the United States, at least my part of it, was founded on a rock; I might forget that four of my ancestors landed from the little ship "Mayflower," and be tempted to follow strange gods unless I had some forceful, though symbolical, reminder close at hand.

We carried our friends' good wishes for us in our undertaking, even though some of them quietly intimated that the pioneer conditions of life and education in the Middle West, for such they were supposed to be at that time, would not hold us long from the well-tried and highly approved mores of the Athens of America. But we were confident and light hearted. Even Mr. Hale's remark as we sped through the Berkshire forests, "Goodbye, Trees," failed to give us concern.

When we reached Hyde Park station the following afternoon, we were met by J. Laurence Laughlin, our old friend and associate. He waved a magazine in the air as he approached us on the platform, and said, "We have a real University; here is the student paper!" Ten days before the University opened!

We drove to the Hotel Monroe on Monroe, later Kenwood, Avenue, just north of Fifty-fifth Street, where we found a few of our new associates had already arrived; and soon we were all settled at dinner, one of the most extraordinary combinations of food I ever saw. We had barely finished when President Harper arrived and I met him for the first time, for he had appointed me on Mrs. Palmer's advice. There was, of course, no opportunity for intimate talk. One reason was that he had brought with him a student who had just appeared at his house, Elizabeth Messick. She had arrived that afternoon at the Union Station from Memphis, Tennessee. As was the custom, not only in Memphis, but in Podunk and Boston, she took a "hack," had her trunk strapped on behind, and told the driver to take her to the Hotel Beatrice at the University of Chicago. Then the journey began. They drove and they drove. Night began to fall. City sights gradually disappeared and were replaced by bits of open country. Fully aware

Alice Freeman Palmer

of the perils lying in wait for a young girl in the wicked city of Chicago, she made eager inquiries of the driver as to how much farther they had to go; but his assurances that they would soon arrive, even though frequently repeated, did not deter her from making ready to leap from the vehicle, speed across the prairie, and disappear in the dusk. In about an hour, the driver thought they were somewhere near the University, but he had to make inquiries, as he had never been there. It was, in fact, several years before the University actually got on the local map—years before it was on the academic map. Having located the University, consisting then of four unfinished buildings— Cobb Hall and three men's residence halls, or "dormitories" as they were called—the next problem was to find the Hotel Beatrice, the only clue being that it was on Fifty-seventh Street. The first attempt proved, on inquiry, to be the Hyde Park High School, which later gave way to a series of other schools, public and parochial. Of course, the schoolhouse was closed and dark. Finally, the Hotel Beatrice was located; but it, too, was closed and dark and not even completely finished. What could be done? The young southerner, with a wit which justified her attempting to enrol as a student in a great University, said, "Let us find out where the President lives—it must be near here." A drug store was found at the corner of Fifty-seventh Street near the railroad, and it was learned that the President lived just around the corner on Washington, later Blackstone, Avenue. Soon the journey was over. The President was somewhat disconcerted to discover that an actual student, an attractive young woman at that, had deposited herself on his front doorstep. Even if never again, he took great satisfaction on that occasion in the fact that he had two women deans at hand to help him out of his difficulty. And so he came to call on his new Faculty, not alone, but with a tall, slender young girl, clad in a circular cape and small cap with a patent-leather visor, her cheeks glowing with excitement and her large dark eyes nearly popping out of her head. There was no room in the little hotel for her, but she had to be housed, so the landlord said he would put a cot for her in the alcove in my room. This suited her so well that, taking advantage of the intimacy thus started, she hardly let me out of her sight for days except when I was at a Faculty or Council meeting or peremptorily engaged in some University duty where she would have been distinctly *de trop.*

It was not long before we moved into our new quarters, the Hotel Beatrice on Fifty-seventh Street. Our experiences there make a tale in themselves and a unique feature in the establishment of a University. While Mrs. Palmer and I were trying to get some order out of the domestic chaos in which we found ourselves, the little group of students busied themselves by day, and even by night, getting ready for their entrance examinations, just as students were accustomed to do in the old-time colleges of the East. These examinations were an innovation in the Middle West, but it did not take much time or effort for the students to create the conventional atmosphere of dread and excitement or to adopt very foolish and wasteful ways of preparing themselves to meet the tests. The examinations were taken; and after a due period of suspense, word came that all of our group at the Beatrice were admitted to the University.

Laying Foundations

The academic system with which Boston was familiar was firmly established. Training for the so-called "learned professions," primarily the ministry and only very lately the law, medicine, and teaching, was its goal. The traditions which had grown up were almost sacrosanct. It is true that President Eliot's bomb, the elective system, had created some disturbance and aroused consternation for fear that this precious heirloom from the past, the college, should be ruined. And Johns Hopkins University with its new program of graduate work had excited interest as something novel but not very pertinent to the situation in hand. Wellesley College and Smith College had seen no other way to open educational opportunities to women than by the path which had been laid out by men. Boston University had opened its doors not very long before to both sexes on equal terms. This was done in the face of the declaration by a distinguished Boston physician that "identical education of the two sexes is a crime before God and humanity that physiology protests against and that experience weeps over. It defies the Roman maxim which physiology has fully justified, *'mens sana in corpore sano.'*"

In spite of this step of admitting women, which was considered very radical in the East, even Boston University did not dare venture far from the well-worn road. The New England colleges had the same list of subjects for admission, practically the same entrance examinations, with very slight variations the same curriculum, and closed their halls for three months in the year. No far-reaching changes in the system had taken place for generations.

It is not strange that the stories of the new venture in the West stirred interest and provoked criticism which ran even into ridicule.

Among the articles of incorporation of the new University of Chicago was the following: "To provide, impart, and furnish opportunities for all departments of higher education to persons of both sexes on equal terms."

The Faculty, on much larger salaries than usual, had been summoned not only from all sections of the United States—Maine to California —but from Canada, Germany, Scotland, and England. They came from Harvard, Cornell, Wisconsin, Princeton, Minnesota, Columbia—from most of the leading colleges, in fact— while eight had held presidencies of colleges or universities. Of these persons, eighteen are (1936) still connected with the University, and four of them are giving active service. The esteem in which an appointment to the new Faculty was held may be shown in part—certainly, in an amusing way—by the academic record of one member of the Faculty, a young Scotsman:

A.M., pass degree, 1883, A.M., Honors of the First Class, 1886, University of Edinburgh; First place on the Honors List, with Bruce of Grangehill Fellowship, 1886; Student at Jena, Paris, Cambridge, Berlin, Freiburg; Ferguson Scholarship (open to honors-men of all Scottish Universities), 1887; Assistant Professor of Logic, Edinburgh University, 1888–90; Locumtenens Professor of the Moral Sciences, Cardiff, for Winter term of 1888; Sir William Hamilton Fellow, Edinburgh, 1888, for three years; Shaw Fellow, 1890, for five years; Lecturer of University Association for Education of Women, Edinburgh, 1889; Government Examiner for Degrees in the Moral Sciences, St. Andrews University, 1890, for three years; Lecturer on Logic and Methodology, Sage School of Philosophy, Cornell University, 1891–2.

The crowning academic glory of his career was that he then became "Tutor in Political Economy, the University of Chicago."

Forty-three fellows were appointed for the first year, of whom six were women.

There were, moreover, other new features which struck the attention of the educational world:

1. The University was to be in continuous session throughout the year, with graduation quarterly. The new President admitted that such a plan would destroy entirely the class spirit, but he also affirmed that there was a certain kind of class spirit which ought to be destroyed.

2. The University was orgianized with four divisions quite new in the university world. In addition to the usual academic divisions, the new features were: (*a*) the University Extension Division, which for a considerable length of time functioned on a large scale; (*b*) the University Libraries, Laboratories, and Museums; (*c*) the University Press; (*d*) the University Affiliations, which included the work done in connection with institutions entering into the relationship of affiliation with the University.

3. Courses of instruction were classed as majors and minors. The former called for ten, eleven, or twelve hours of classroom instruction each week; the latter, for half as many hours. Normal work for a student was to be two courses, one major and one minor. The tuition fee for this amount of instruction was $25.00 a quarter. Incidentally, it is interesting to note that table board was to be from $3.00 to $4.00 a week and rooms in the dormitories from $1.50 to $3.00 a week.

4. Although the certificate system of admission was practiced by all large middle western universities, entrance examinations were to be held three times a year in twenty different cities and were required of all students. These examinations were divided into six groups. Latin, English, history, one modern language,

and mathematics were common to them all. There was a choice offered between Greek, science, and more modern language; otherwise there was no election.

5. The Colleges of Arts, of Literature, and of Science were each divided into an Academic College and a University College, or, as they were later known, a Junior College and a Senior College. The requirements in each college were quite distinct. In the Academic Colleges definite curricula were outlined, and there was no election. In the University Colleges a student took not more than one-half his work in one department and all of his work in not more than four departments.

6. Mr. Rockefeller's first gift ($600,000), made in May, 1889, was toward an endowment fund for a college in Chicago. It was stated later that it had never been the purpose of the American Baptist Education Society to seek to limit the institution to the work of a college. It was not long before, under the guidance of Professor Harper, plans for a university began to take shape. Mr. Rockefeller's second gift, of $1,000,000, in September, 1890, contained the stipulation that the income of $800,000 should be used for non-professional graduate instruction and fellowships. In a statement intended to be a part of his first annual report to the Board of Trustees, President Harper, as he had then become, wrote:

It is expected by all who are interested that the University idea is to be emphasized. It is proposed to establish not a college, but a university. . . . It has been the desire to establish an institution which should not be a rival with the many colleges already in existence, but an institution which should help those colleges. . . .

It is only the man who has made investigation who may teach others to investigate. . . . In other words, it is proposed in this institution to make the work of investigation primary, the work of giving instruction secondary.

7. Lecturers and teachers were to be classified as follows: (*a*) the head professor, (*b*) the professor, (*c*) the professor, non-resident, (*d*) the associate professor, (*e*) the assistant professor, (*f*) the instructor, (*g*) the tutor, (*h*) the docent, (*i*) the reader, (*j*) the lecturer, (*k*) the fellow, (*l*) the scholar.

8. Professors were not required to give more than eight or ten hours a week to classroom work, thus making it possible for them to carry on investigation all the time.

9. When the number of students necessitated it, courses were to be duplicated, one section being open to students of grades A, B, and C, and the other to students of grades D and E.

10. To promote more advanced study and individual research, and to bring together instructors and students, seminars were to be organized in various departments of the Colleges. Academic College and University College seminars were to be distinct in the same department.

11. Students were to be examined as to their physical condition on entering and at intervals during their course, and were required to take four half-hours a week of class work in physical culture throughout their course.

12. It was evidently anticipated that certain time-hallowed customs of eastern colleges would prevail in the new institution, judging from the fact that a bond of $200 was required of each student, guaranteeing payment of bills and "such sums as may be charged for damage to University property caused by the student's act or neglect."

13. In general, an assistant dean was to be appointed for every one hundred students in a division.

Brief and incomplete as this sketch is, it seems clear why those Boston friends of the academic adventurers were fearful and why a bit of the rock on which New England was founded was given as a talisman. It looked almost as if the whole rock might be needed!

What happened to the new scheme? The quarter system has

not only remained in force but has been widely copied. University extension lecture study was abandoned for various causes in 1911, but correspondence study for many years gained steadily in scope and enrolment. The University Press had become an increasingly useful and influential division of the University. The University Affiliations have become less and less formal and mechanical in character, while in general effectiveness they have gained.

Entrance examinations were maintained for several years, the number of subjects being increased and conditions amounting to three of the fifteen units being allowed. In the announcement for 1898–99 there appeared for the first time the statement that subject certificates from affiliated and co-operating schools would be accepted. The University has found itself unable, single-handed, to maintain the entrance examinations. The announcement for 1915–16 indicated another fundamental change. The high schools had been growing more and more discontented with the dominance assumed by the colleges and the policies dictated by them in regard to high-school curricula. At this juncture the University of Chicago decided to receive from approved schools any student graduating with an average grade higher than the passing mark of the school, provided the student offered three units of English and two subjects which had been studied intensively. Otherwise, within rather wide but specified limits, the student might offer any courses accepted by the school for graduation.

The last major of the original type disappeared after the announcement for 1897–98, but the principle of intensive studying of a few subjects has not only been continued but has been developed. It has never been possible for a student to take such a course as I had in my Senior year, viz., Italian, two hours weekly; Metaphysics, three; Calculus, two; Evidences of Christianity, three; Greek, two; Geology, three.

After many modifications in the courses of study required for the degree, the principle of continuation and distribution groups of subjects in the Junior Colleges and of intensive work in two fields, i.e., principal and secondary sequences, in the Senior Colleges was adopted in 1912.

Moreover, I had found that much of the listless drifting of the women students could be prevented and many a rather dreary college course of doubtful educational value could be converted into one of interest and real value if each student could be induced early in the course to choose a vocation and arrange her studies with reference to it. At my request a special committee was appointed to study the situation and, as the result, the rigid regulations were greatly modified, especially for students entered with advanced standing. They were given the choice of specific sequences or of presenting an acceptable and rational scheme of courses to be followed up to graduation. The so-called New Plan now in effect has done away with many absurd and wasteful practices under the older systems. Its ultimate value remains to be proved, but it is a great satisfaction to me to realize that my successors do not have to sit almost weekly on Saturday mornings arguing about grade points, and possible exceptions to the detailed rules in regard to the curriculum. At the time we thought the procedure was inevitable if the welfare and intellectual growth of students were deemed of concern to the Faculty.

A few more changes from the original plans may be noted:

The classification of the teaching staff has been greatly reduced. The unhappy head professor was among those to disappear. Sectioning students by ability has not been effectively put into operation. Its uses as a subject for Faculty discussion and controversy are not yet exhausted. The undergraduate seminars never took form except on paper. The requirements in physical education have been, to my mind, unfortunately abandoned, while, on the other hand, there is more medical supervision and advice.

The $200 bond disappeared in 1896. By that time it had been made perfectly clear that certain types of so-called "college spirit" manifesting itself in destruction of property would be no part of the life at the University of Chicago.

The ratio of one dean to each hundred students was not long maintained. It soon became one to two hundred, and remained at about that point until the great influx of students after the World War, when it became about one to three hundred.

In 1892–93 the total number of students was 744, of whom 306, or over 40 per cent, were college graduates. Students were enrolled the first year from thirty-three states and twelve foreign countries. The courage of these students in joining the new venture was a marvel, and in some measure proved that its plans met a genuine need.

The Physical Education Department started out with much éclat. The prestige of Mr. Stagg in some respects surpassed that of any other member of the Faculty. Certainly more eyes were turned upon him as he walked through Cobb Hall. His efforts to establish a football team met with success, but unfortunately a scandal in connection with the sport soon caused the University a great deal of trouble. A man was admitted to the University as a special or unclassified student and was immediately put on the team. The day after the final game he left the University, having given ample evidence that he was not a student and had no intention of being one. This, with other incidents, showed Mr. Stagg that the whole sport needed overhauling and new methods devised for conducting it. The first step proposed at a Faculty meeting was to refuse to allow any but regular college students to take part on University teams. I immediately foresaw that trouble might arise from having women, not really students, enter as unclassified students, enrol for a course in French or literature, and then claim the right to participate in all student activities, such as the glee club and dramatic club; so I asked that the rule be made to cover both sexes. It served a good purpose many times in eliminating so-called "students" who had no interest in the real advantages of the University, and at the same time making the various activities really collegiate without the harmful influences of professionalism.

J. Laurence Laughlin   Alonzo A. Stagg

Albion W. Small

The practical administration of the University was, of course, a matter of the first importance. President Harper was continually working over methods for its improvement. He delighted in visualizing the interrelation of its different parts. It was something like a jig-saw puzzle. I remember vividly how at a meeting he interrupted the discussion to sketch on a paper how one part was subordinated to another—a committee to a Board, a Board to a Faculty, a Faculty on one hand to the Senate, and on the other to the University Council, and these to the Trustees. Where was the President? He jocosely (or perhaps seriously) said one day, "Between the upper and nether millstones."

The story of his choice of a teaching staff is told in detail in Dr. T. W. Goodspeed's *History of the University of Chicago*. It shows how high a standard for education in the Middle West he intended to set. In spite of the high salaries offered ($7,000 for a head professor), many noted scholars were reluctant to leave assured positions for what, in spite of President Harper's confidence and optimism, might prove to be a dream university. There can be no doubt that those who accepted the challenge never regretted their decision.

The summons for the first official Faculty meeting which followed many months of preliminary organization was like a clarion call to those who appreciated its significance.

A sheet of paper headed simply, "The University of Chicago," and printed in light-blue ink carried this message crudely mimeographed to the sixty men and women, more or less, who constituted the first Faculty of Arts, Literature, and Science of the new University of Chicago:

SEPT. 28, 1892

Dear Sir: You are invited by the President to meet the Faculty of Arts, Literature, and Science on Saturday, October 1, at 4:30 p.m. at Room A 7.

Recorder

It may be noted that the building was not designated. There was no need. Cobb Hall it must have been, since there was no other building save the three men's residence halls to the south. Even Cobb Hall was unfinished, lacking a front door, and was entered by means of walking over the threshold on a plank.

"Room A 7" was the large room at the southeast corner of the first floor. For many years it was known as "the Faculty room"; and in that room, with President Harper's office adjoining, were born and nurtured or, after trial, discarded those policies which were fruit of the extraordinary vision of the young President and the varied experiences of his Faculty. The room was not merely large but attractive, with leather-covered chairs, a long center table, and rugs agreeable to the eye—a room quite different from the hit-or-miss quarters familiar to most of these newcomers as places where business must be hurried in order to escape to a more congenial environment.

Some of the members of the University Faculties had themselves formerly been accustomed to preside at their own staff meetings: Ezekial G. Robinson, of Brown University; George W. Northrup, of the Baptist Union Theological Seminary; Galusha Anderson, of the old University of Chicago and of Denison University; Thomas C. Chamberlin, of the University of Wisconsin; Alice Freeman Palmer, of Wellesley College; and Albion W. Small, of Colby University. From many parts of the world members of this group came to cast in their lot with the new institution under its stimulating and enthusiastic leader. Several were from Germany, from England and Scotland, while great universities— Harvard, Yale, Johns Hopkins, Michigan, Wisconsin, Minnesota, Illinois, California—gave their quotas. Here took place the first of that series of mighty word-battles between Professor T. C. Chamberlin and Professor W. G. Hale on the relative importance of the classics and the sciences which continued as long as the two men met to discuss educational policies, or any other question, in fact!

The University of Chicago

Weekly Bulletin for the Week
Closing Friday, October 14.

FRIDAY, 12:30 P. M. Chapel Service, Rev. P. S. Henson, D. D.
Theme: "The Great Teacher."

SATURDAY, 12:30 P. M. Chapel Service.

SUNDAY, 9 A. M. Religious Service in the Chapel

4:00 P. M. University lecture: The Book of Job: The
First Cycle of Speeches, Chaps. iv-xiv. By the President

MONDAY, 12:30 P. M. Chapel Service, Rev. L. P. Mercer, D. D.
Theme: "The Divine Life in Human Form"

" 4:30 P. M. Meeting of the Divinity Faculty.

TUESDAY, 12:30 P. M. Chapel Service, Rev. J. H. Barrows, D. D.
Theme: "Fellowship in the Spiritual Life."

WEDNESDAY, 12:30 P. M. Chapel Service.

" 3:00 P. M. Biological Club. Theme: "General
Physiology and its Relation to Morphology." *

4:30 P. M. University Extension Lecture: Prof. Moulton,
"Faust on Easter Eve: the Temptation Internal."

THURSDAY, 12:30 P. M. Chapel Service.

" 4:30 P. M. Lecture, by Prof. W. I. Knapp: "The
Life and Times of Cervantes." University Hall.

" 7:30 P. M. The Semitic Club, 5657 Washington Ave.

" 7:30 P. M. The Divinity School Literary Society in
Lecture Hall.

FRIDAY, 12:30 P. M. Chapel Service.

FRIDAY, 4:30 P. M. Meeting of the Faculty of Arts, Literature
and Science.

* These meetings are intended primarily for the biological faculty and fellows Students
in biology are invited to attend.

VOL. 1   NO. 1   MAY 7 · 14

THE OFFICIAL BULLETIN
O F
The University of Chicago.

GENERAL STATEMENT.

The Official Bulletin of the University of Chicago will be issued under the direction of the University Council every Saturday morning. It will contain (1) standing announcements of the regular meetings of the various Faculties, Boards and University Organizations, (2) special notices from the Administrative offices which concern Faculties or students, (3) special announcements for the following week, including chapel addresses, lectures, meetings of the various clubs and other University Organizations.

The Subscription price is one dollar per year (twenty-five cents for the remainder of the Quarter). Subscriptions should be paid at the Registrar's Office.

All notices for the Bulletin must be handed in at the Recorder's Office before Thursday noon of each week in order to find place in the Bulletin issued on the following Saturday.

ANNOUNCEMENTS.

SUNDAY.

LECTURE.—*Zephaniah.* PRES. WILLIAM R. HARPER. This lecture is the first of a series of eight lectures on the Prophecies connected with the Fall of Jerusalem. *Chapel, Cobb Lecture Hall, 4:00 P. M.*

THE CHRISTIAN UNION.—*Belief and Analytical Study.* MR. WILLIAM CALDWELL. *Chapel, Cobb Lecture Hall, 7:30 P. M.*

TUESDAY.

GENERAL MEETING OF THE DIVINITY SCHOOL. —PROF. GEORGE W. NORTHRUP, leader. *Chapel, Cobb Lecture Hall, 4:00 P. M.*

WEDNESDAY.

Last day for notifications from candidates for the degrees of A.M. and Ph.D.

Rehearsal of the University Chorus, *Chapel of Cobb Lecture Hall, 4:00 P. M.*

MEETING OF THE POLITICAL SCIENCE CLUB: Address: *The Early Legal History of Illinois,*

MR. C. C. PICKETT, *Faculty Room, Cobb Lecture Hall, 7:30 P. M.*

THURSDAY.

MEETING OF THE MATHEMATICAL CLUB.— Subject: *Concerning the Transformation of Hyperelliptic Integrals to Elliptic Integrals,* MR. HUTCHINSON. *Room 17 C, 2:30 P. M.*

THE DIVINITY FACULTY meets in the Faculty Room at 4:00 P. M.

COMMENCEMENT EXERCISES OF SWEDISH DIVISION OF THE DIVINITY SCHOOL.—*Cobb Lecture Hall, at 8:00 P. M.*

FRIDAY.

LAST DAY OF THE FIRST TERM OF THE SPRING QUARTER.

THE UNIVERSITY COUNCIL meets in the Faculty Room at 4:00. P. M.

SPRING MEETING OF THE UNIVERSITY UNION. *Cobb Lecture Hall, 8:00 P. M.*

SATURDAY.

SECOND TERM OF THE SPRING QUARTER BEGINS.

Such was the setting for that first Faculty meeting. What happened? The official record is meager. Dr. Charles R. Henderson, the Recorder, was dearly beloved; but his gifts lay in a different direction from that of taking detailed minutes of a meeting. Possibly, too, realizing the significance of the occasion, his power of expression was benumbed somewhat, as happens when one is called by long-distance telephone from halfway across the continent. Fortunately, some private notes taken at the time help fill out the picture. Practically all of the Faculty were present, as it was too thrilling an occasion to miss.

President Harper opened the meeting with prayer, and this

continued to be his custom whether official gatherings were large or small. He then, in the words of the Minutes, "gave a brief address upon some special points for consideration." The President emphasized the importance of securing unity in spirit, but not necessarily in opinion, as the members of the group organized and developed the institution. He said that the burdens involved in the preliminary organization had been carried by a few and must henceforth be borne by the many. He described in general terms the lines of separation between the Senate, the Council, and the Faculty. The several duties and responsibilities of these bodies, he thought, would have to be more fully defined as the result of experience; but he urged that flexibility should always be their characteristic. Several specific topics were mentioned for discussion; but he dwelt chiefly upon secret societies and their place in the University, reported that the Trustees had already had the subject under discussion, and presented the following suggestions to the Faculty:

1. The rules of each society, the location of its rooms, etc., should be made known.

2. Special emphasis should be placed on literary societies.

3. Societies detrimental to the interests of the University should be given up or disbanded.

4. Restrictions as to membership might be possible.

It was "moved by Mr. Howland that under the restrictions named by the President secret societies be permitted in the University." "On motion of Mr. Laughlin this matter was committed to a committee for consideration." The President named in this committee Messrs. Judson, Hale, Small, Tufts, and Stagg.

A plan for a University bulletin was announced, and it was stated that on Thursday at noon of each week the material for announcements for the weekly bulletin should be handed to the Recorder.

The Examiner, Mr. Abbott, reported that 510 students had been matriculated, divided as follows: Graduate School, 126; Colleges, in three upper classes, 85; Colleges, in Freshman class, 85; special students, 61; Divinity School, 153—a total of 510.

"The President expresses the hope that the time will come when the Academy College work may be transferred to some other place and the higher work be given all our strength on this campus." The meeting then adjourned, having revealed several outstanding figures and started the discussion of questions which, after more than forty years, are not yet fully settled. Best of all was the strengthening of enthusiasm and confidence in the venture with which the members had cast in their lots. The significance of the spirit which prevailed cannot be fully understood without some knowledge of the strong personalities involved and their individual characteristics. There was laid the foundation of the feeling of unity and devotion which prevailed through the following years not only in this highly responsible group but throughout the University, and, with few exceptions, in every member of it, even to the humblest. A simple incident will illustrate this: A young scullery maid employed in the Kelly Hall kitchen left her work of paring potatoes one day to go, on the invitation of a friend, to a cooking lesson in the city. On her return she was asked how she had enjoyed herself. "My," she said, "I've learned more than I've learned all the time I've been in the University!" Even the basement of Kelly Hall was the University; and every task, even the simplest, was a share in its making. "In the University" was the all-pervading spirit.

The incidents which have been narrated are but as veneer in comparison with the real substance of the University in those early years. The keynote was struck in the President's offices, where, under the gracious and yet amazingly discreet guidance of Miss Cobb, the President's amanuensis, a crowd was always to be found during his office hours, bringing their problems, small and large, to him for answer, or else responding to his numerous calls for conference. At one of these he said to me, "I sometimes take the other side so as to hear what can be said—I agree with you." Each visitor noted on a slip of paper the business he had in mind. The procession moved rapidly; but there was no sense of pressure, and it was very seldom that anyone left the office without a feeling of satisfaction, even if the answer had been unfavorable. Every member of his staff was made to feel that his relationship to his chief was personal, not merely official.

This was true of students also. Individual conferences and consultation with groups tended to build up an extraordinary sense of unity. The gatherings of prospective candidates for advanced degrees for a matutinal breakfast at his house on Convocation Day, the student councils whose meetings and policies interested him greatly, the congregation whose membership included not only Faculty but Doctors of the University, the Convocation receptions, where a special welcome was given to the relatives and friends of the graduating students—these, and many other ways to whose success Mrs. Harper contributed generously, built up a spirit which was quite unique. It certainly struck my mother in that way, for she recalled how my brother, up to the time of his graduation from Harvard College, had never met President Eliot. Visitors to the University, familiar with conditions in academic communities, often commented on the harmony and loyalty which prevailed at Chicago. It was amply shown that kindness and friendliness, and even a certain amount of informality, were not inconsistent with conventional standards of social intercourse. I was told once by an academic official of wide experience that the official manners of the University of Chicago were the best in the country. It was clearly understood that not only in the President's office were visitors to be received with courtesy, but everyone desiring help or information in any office and seeking them in a suitable way were to find the open door and understanding word. This extended even to clerks, who took the cue from the officers they represented. I am free to confess, however, that I was sometimes deeply offended when I realized that I was recognized as an officer of the University and, as such, received more courteous treatment than would have been the case if I had appeared as a stranger. But on the whole, visitors to the University were given the feeling that their interest was appreciated and not considered an obnoxious intrusion.

Amenities

A generation passes in the public mind as a long period. A college generation is a different matter. One follows another very rapidly, and with each succeeding one the recent past becomes more and more indistinct and its achievements and characteristics lose reality and pass into the realm of tradition. This has happened in the case of the first president of the University, who at the age of thirty-four was officially elected to the position. In less than a normal generation President Harper has become practically a myth to the present college world. There are even young students at the University who do not know for whom the great memorial library building is named. Among others, the knowledge may be widespread that he was a man with profound educational insight and imagination, seconded with organizing genius, creative energy, tremendous vitality and industry, and extraordinary skill as a teacher. But other traits, perhaps more human but which contributed to his success and also to the devotion and affection which he won from his associates, have passed almost wholly into the shadows. A few incidents showing these traits are worth noting. Although bred simply, and modest in his personal habits, he craved satisfaction for his aesthetic tastes in music and other forms of art. As a youth he played the cornet in his hometown band; and, even at the beginning of the University, he encouraged the establishment of an orchestra by the students. He not infrequently referred to his hope that the University might some day have a great graduate school of music under the direction of Theodore Thomas. He had a fine piano in his home; and friends, sometimes world-renowned musicians, often came to play to him. Even modest skill served to meet his craving, as the following note shows:

MY DEAR MISS TALBOT:

It is quite a lonely place over here. Could you not bring over some of your music, and play a little this evening? It is more than probable that you have an engagement—but if not, perhaps you will come.

Yours very sincerely,

[Signed] William R. Harper

Of course, I responded at once. Armed with selections from Beethoven, Schubert, and Mendelssohn, I crossed the street from Green Hall and seated myself at the piano, which almost played itself, while he stretched himself out on a lounge, evidently in great fatigue; but a quiet adagio movement from Beethoven, very simply played, soon brought sounds of heavy breathing. A more skilled pianist and a different type of music would probably have had another effect. Greatly pleased, as well as amused with the effect of my performance, I did not dare stop even to turn a page of my music sheets, but played over and over the same sweet notes whose soft melodious sounds were accompanied by the gradually increasing noise of his breathing, which, after awhile—there is no evading the fact—changed to an actual snore! With this, the performance ended. He had awakened himself and, after he had thanked me warmly and apologized heartily, I left with the hope that life might bring me many opportunities to render simple services so fruitful in good.

He had a remarkable way of stimulating one to attempt what seemed impossible. I recall his sending for me once and saying, "There is to be a meeting of about two hundred Baptist ministers here tomorrow. Would it be possible to have luncheon for them at Kelly Hall." Of course it would—there could no longer be a question in his mind or in mine, and it would be fun to do it—but how, with an equipment for forty, was my part of the question to be solved; but solved it was!

One characteristic of President Harper was not known generally to the world but was familiar to those who came in personal contact with him, and did much to establish cordial and friendly relations between him and his associates instead of the formal and perfunctory dealings which might otherwise have arisen from their official connection. His manner was always simple and kind and courteous, no matter how great the honors and responsibilities poured upon him by the world. And his acts did not belie his words. It seemed hardly credible that such a heavy load of care could permit of so many deeds of kindness. When word came to me of my mother's death, he was with me in a few minutes after I had sent word that I was starting for the East, and his tender and sympathetic expressions were a great comfort. If I were to notify him that I was starting on a vacation trip, or going to a meeting of the Association of Collegiate Alumnae, back would have come the message, "Go and have a good time." When one accomplished something creditably, there was sure to come from him a message of commendation and encouragement. These are simple illustrations of his kindness. Many more important ones could be cited, but they would mean no more.

In the early years religious exercises were held daily in what was called the Chapel, which occupied the whole of the north end of the first floor of Cobb Hall. I was asked to be one of a group to take turns in officiating at these exercises. In great perturbation I went to President Harper and told him that I had never conducted religious exercises and I feared this new duty, added to the heavy load I was already carrying, would prove too much. He immediately reassured me and said that I might be excused. He added, "With all the experience I have had in the conduct of religious services, I never close such a meeting without feeling that I have been through a severe strain." And yet, this was the man whom I met all aglow as he came from a class and who said, "I have just had such a wonderful time. I could not carry this administrative work if it were not for my teaching."

A different type of illustration of his simple, direct manner is seen in his preference to be called "Mr." rather than "Doctor" or "President." Indeed, it was not until the next administration that the head of the institution was addressed generally as "President." But Dr. Harper had been called "Doctor" so much that the term clung to him after he became President, though his family, in general, kept to the simpler term. He established the custom that, although the University had established many different academic ranks (twelve, in fact), no social differences were recognized by title, and "Mr." was the term generally approved and commonly used when addressing the men of the Faculty. The *University of Chicago Weekly*, Volume I, No. 1, published two weeks before the day the University opened, contained this statement: "By mutual agreement between all the faculty and officers of the University now on hand, the uniform appellation of 'Mr.' has been adopted in mutual intercourse, thus doing away with all doubts and mistakes as to the proper title of any man connected with the institution." Indeed, about the only times when one heard an inquiry about "Professor So and So" were when somebody visited the University and tried to find this "professor" and he proved to be a graduate student who had always been known as" professor" to his students in the high school. [. . .]

In striking contrast to some of his qualities were his love of form, color, and ceremony. These were shown in the life of the University in the importance placed on academic costume, use of the University color, and the formalities in public exercises, which were an innovation in the Middle West. The cap and gown were introduced at the beginning, the type being a modification of the usual English style. The following letter, dated October 12, 1892, was sent out by the President:

At a meeting of the Board of Trustees of the University of Chicago, it was voted to request the wearing of the official cap and gown by the professors and students of the University on the following occasions:

1. On all occasions on which degrees are conferred or honors bestowed—by professors and students participating in the exercises.

2. At all final examinations for high degrees—by professors and students present.

3. At the regular chapel service—by those who conduct the service or sit upon the platform.

4. At all formal meetings of the Faculties, the University Council and the University Senate.

5. At all public lectures delivered by instructors of the University at the University, and at public lectures delivered by instructors of the University outside of the University in such cases as the instructor may deem best.

6. By students on all public exhibitions.

7. At all official University receptions.

It has been decided that there shall be five distinct gowns namely, (1) for head professors and professors; (2) for associate professors and assistant professors; (3) for instructors to docents inclusive; (4) for fellows; (5) for students. Inclosed will be found a statement of the prices at which gowns will be furnished by two firms, one in Chicago and one in Albany.

I remain,

Yours very truly,

[*Signed*] *William R. Harper*

It would be difficult to say how much influence the University had in bringing about a uniform system for the United States, but it was not long before the academic world adopted a series of colors designating different faculties, and styles of gowns, sleeves, and hoods showing different degrees, while the color of the lining of the hood indicated the institution from which the degree was taken. Gold tassels on the cap, showing administrative position, added a final touch to the picturesqueness of the system which, in the opinion of the unbelievers, was far from being a symbol of "Pure Thought." But there were some members of the Faculties, even very learned men, who took delight in the system, especially in proportion as, with the multiplication of degrees held by a single person, its application became more intricate. I shall never forget the intense absorption of Rabbi Hirsch in the problem of how to combine in one costume the colors of the many degrees, honorary and others, he had received. Even with the help of the dealer's agent and several colleagues it was a puzzle, but it was finally solved to his evident satisfaction. Of course, the President's combination was intricate also.

As time passed, however, the regulations governing the use of the cap and gown were gradually relaxed. It would be more exact to say that they were ignored. It did not take many experiences like conducting a three-hour doctor's examination in a classroom with the thermometer over ninety degrees, or standing in the street under a broiling hot summer sun waiting to escort Mr. Rockefeller, to persuade the majority of the faculties that there were occasions when the wearing of the voluminous heavy robes was far from an ideal of comfort and not an essential factor in high scholarship. The expense also was a serious difficulty in the opinion of many. So it came about that the cap and gown were seen only on rare and the most official occasions; but to many friends and observers, next to the actual awarding of degrees, the most exciting feature of the Convocation exercises has always been the colorful procession, especially when it included the scarlet robes of English or Canadian universities or the even more picturesque academic costumes of other foreign countries.

The color of the University was originally old gold, but how or when it was chosen does not seem to be on record. Newspaper jibes and other annoying circumstances made a change desirable, and in 1894 maroon was substituted. To the uninitiated it would not seem a difficult or important matter to decide. But it involved many meetings of committees and Council, correspondence with Harvard, Illinois, Wisconsin, and other institutions, to avoid conflict with their colors, consideration of the needs of the Athletic Department, the fitness of the name for song and cheering purposes and for decoration— in fact, a very serious and important step was involved. The result was satisfactory, especially when members of the University were not too particular about choosing for their purposes a shade of red that could hardly be called "maroon."

The original color for the lining of the doctor's hood was royal purple, and an official sample was kept. It became increasingly difficult to match this shade, even when stores dealing in ecclesiastical goods were visited. Even the women of the faculty who had to do the buying found it difficult to realize how many shades of purple there could be. When the color of the University became the color for the lining of the hood, there seemed to be less difficulty, perhaps because the exact shade of maroon did not seem to matter so much.

Even from the beginning, a rather unwonted formality marked the different official functions. To some this formality seemed to verge on pagan ceremonial rites; but to most there was a sense of satisfaction in the dignity and order with which the functions were conducted. Naturally, well-trained assistants were needed to accomplish this; and as the number of participants increased, it was found that some help, other than that which the Faculty could give, was necessary. It was decided that the student body could be drawn from and the appointments made a mark of great distinction. At the Ninth Convocation, held June 2, 1895, one marshal, four assistant marshals, and twenty-two ushers, all men students, served as aides. The ushers disappeared after the Twelfth Convocation. It was soon pointed out that the distinction might well be bestowed on women also. On the program for the Thirty-second Convocation, held April 2, 1900, the list of newly appointed marshals included the names of Marian Harmon Calhoun and Mary Ethel Freeman. Their names appeared on succeeding Convocation programs, including that of the Thirty-eighth Convocation, held on June 18, 1901, when they received their degrees; but during this time Miss Calhoun declined to appear as an assistant marshal. No small incident could show more vividly the social changes which were soon to take place in the position of women than the reason given, which was that the public appearances required were not in accord with the modesty and refinement which marked a well-bred lady! Following this experience, only men marshals were appointed until the system was adopted which differentiated the women from the men. At the Fifty-third Convocation, held December 20, 1904, in addition to ten college marshals, six women were appointed as college aides. Somewhat later, the number of appointments became the same for both men and women, and the system has been continuous and very successful. The aides so greatly enjoyed their duties and privileges that an informal type of organization gradually developed. Annual reunions and dinners are held at which the newly appointed aides are introduced to the older ones and interesting personal and official experiences are recounted.

It must not be thought that life in the University, organized or unorganized, was altogether serious. Indeed, many persons will recall amusing incidents and fun-making events more easily than they will official or personal situations of a solemn nature. One of the first of these was a mock seminar given by the students in Cobb Hall on February 22, 1893. The program appeared in the form of a miniature of the official University bulletin. The subscription was announced as free, "single copies 15 cents." The accompanying cut shows the inside pages. It must be remembered that it was issued when preparations were going on rapidly for the World's Columbian Exposition and the study of Browning's

I. THE OFFICER OF ADMINISTRATION.*

A. ALONZO STAGG, PH.D., D.D., LL.D., S.T.D., Dean of the
  Seminar, and Head Professor of AthleticExtension.

> Ph.D., Morgan Park, 1853; D.D., Lake Geneva, 1858; LL.D., Boston
> Latin School, 1862; Senior Wrestler and Reader of McGuffey's First,
> *ibid.*; S.T.D., Wellesley, 1880; Stroke Senior Crew, *ibid.*; Washington
> Fellow at Vassar [open to honorsmen of all American schools], 1886;
> Lecturer Extraordinarius to Home for Incurables, 1887-8.

II. OFFICERS OF GOVERNMENT AND INSTRUCTION.

JESSE D. BURKS, B.L., Docent in Egyptology.

> B.L., University of Paris [Missouri], 1882; Student at Naples Aqua-
> rium, July-August, 1890; Student at Coney Island Sociological Labora-
> tory, Summer of 1891.

LYDIA M. DAME, PH.D., Docent in Hymnology.

> Ph.D., Harvard Annex [degree held in abeyance], 1886; Interpreter to
> the Boston Browning Society, Summer 1889; Docent Emeritus to the
> Board of Lady Managers, Columbian Exposition, 1892.

THEODORO GERALDO SOARES, F.R.S., Advisory Director University Union.

> F.R.S., Business College Cairo [Illinois], 1889; Reader in Pastoral
> Duties, 1890-92 [in same]; Electrical Engineer and Regulator of Ven-
> tilating Fan U. of C. [in absentia], 1892-94.

---

* With the exception of the Dean the names in each group are arranged
in the order of collegiate seniority.

III. THE GRADUATE SCHOOL.

FELLOWS.

LEONARD A. BLUE, A.M., Non-Resident Fellow in Practical
Theology.

A.M., Zürich, 1889; Babylonian Reader to Cook's Excursion, Season
1890; Student in Anthropology, Dime Museum, Chicago, 1891-2; Street
Professor to Chicago Municipal Council, 1892-3.

JOSEPH E. RAYCROFT, A.B., B.D., PH.D., Methodology.

A.B., Texas Wesleyan, 1889; B.D., *ibid.*, 1890; Ph.D., Wesleyan Union
Theological Seminary, 1891; Physical Examiner to Columbian Guides,
and Reader to Columbian School of Wheeled Chairs, 1892-3.

MYRA REYNOLDS, O.N.T., PH.D., Neurasthenia [Americanitis].

O.N.T., Clark University, 1890; Ph.D., Chautauqua College of Liberal
Arts, Summer 1890; Lecturer of University Extension Association for
Education of Men, 1891-2; Fellow by Courtesy [chiefly in Morgan Park]
Summer 1892.

HONORARY FELLOW.

ANN BALDWIN, A.B., Old Testament History.

A.B., Hyde Park H. S., 1880; Corresponding Secretary to Graduate
Association for Promotion of Manners and Morals among Undergraduates, U. of C., 1892-3.

FRANCES WILLISTON, A.B., Practical Politics.

A.B., National University, 1892.

poems was the fashion in women's clubs. But many of the sly pokes at doings of current interest will not be understood except by those who were alive at that time. The theme of the seminar was Washington as a sun myth, and this thesis was proved in a masterly way by Miss Myra Reynolds, then a fellow in the University, who drew upon a fund of etymological and anthropological lore to the complete satisfaction of the audience in the lecture hall on the first floor. The whole performance was a daring and amusing satire not only on the innovations of the University but on the personal peculiarities of some of the Faculty. The myth having been established, the program closed with a serious patriotic appeal given in his characteristically eloquent manner by Mr. Soares. The performance has never been surpassed for genuine cleverness, though there have been some close seconds. One of these was an entertainment in Kent Theater, the largest place of assembly until Mandel Hall was built. The outstanding number was dancing dolls, a forerunner of a popular number in modern shows. The long legs and arms, and their stiff angularity, of Phil Allen and Ray, known later as Professor Philip S. Allen and Dr. Joseph E. Raycroft of Princeton University, brought down the house with gales of laughter and was an often sought-for and generously given feature of entertainments in later years.

Not long afterward came the first of a series of shows with lyrics and dialogue written chiefly, perhaps wholly at first, by members of the Faculty. Again satire and wit held sway, to the great amusement of large audiences; but in time the Faculty withdrew, leaving the field to the students who, organized as the Blackfriars, were often the object of discussion by the Board of Student Organizations, which steadfastly refused permission for performances at a city theater or out of town.

The orchestra, organized the first year, the two glee clubs, and small musical societies under one name or another furnished much pleasure as the years passed. Various persons produced individual stunts: long-legged Charles R. Mann going up and down a tower, Mr. Stagg with amusing songs, Agnes Wayman and Marie Ortmayer as the Cherry Sisters, an Irish story from me in costume, and even not too publicly, a fisticuff match between Dean, and later President, Judson and me were exhibitions which were effective in removing the strain of hard academic and administrative work.

CHAPTER FOUR

Social Life and Mrs. Grundy

Robert Morss Lovett, writing of the first connection with the University of Chicago of his colleague and friend, William Vaughn Moody, said, "The crudeness of the western scene oppressed him sorely," and later on in this article, in the *Atlantic Monthly*, made the statement that "his [Moody's] new environment offered from the beginning an intellectual companionship and stimulus fully as valuable as that which Harvard had to give." These two sentences give a vivid and accurate picture of the heterogeneous conditions in which the members of the new University, Faculty and students alike, found themselves when the University opened in 1892. They were gathered not only from many parts of the United States but from many other parts of the world. They found themselves in a city not yet sixty years old, already overgrown in physical size but with very meager opportunities for education, scholarship, and the amenities of life. In fact, the Stock Yards was the feature of Chicago which most frequently came to people's minds when Chicago was mentioned. Even as late as 1902, when Prince Henry of Prussia visited Chicago, the Stock Yards was its one object of interest known to him and which he expressed a desire to see, although under some pressure he graciously accepted an invitation to visit the University.

A small and encouraging beginning had been made toward an art museum. Mr. Theodore Thomas' influence in music was beginning to be felt; a public library had been started; Hull-House had been established by Jane Addams; certain social customs which were well established in the East were observed by a small circle of people; but Mr. Lovett's phrase, "the somewhat forced and pretentious quality of Chicago's nascent culture," gives an accurate impression of what the newcomers found.

It would have been difficult, however, at that time to believe that within a generation the cultural achievements of the city would attract the wonder and admiration of the entire world, and make quite out of date the phrase added to Bobby Hale's bedtime prayer at Cornell when his father accepted a professorship at Chicago, "Goodbye, God, we are going to Chicago"—God to him meaning "sweetness and light."

One of the first undertakings of the new University was to establish friendly relations with the best and most helpful influences to be found in the city. It was fortunate in winning as friends many of the ablest and most cultured citizens, including Mr. Martin A. Ryerson and Mr. Charles L. Hutchinson, whose generosity and wisdom never failed. It was clear that the University must not fail in its own special type of leadership. What form this should take in regard to the social life of the University, and especially of the women, appeared at once as an important matter for Mrs. Palmer and me to consider. She set about making contacts with the actual and potential friends of the University, while it fell to me to help guide the social activities within its walls. It was necessary to formulate the essential principles of good social form and to decide what social conventions had lost their meaning and should be discarded. A few incidents will show the manifold variety of situations which arose.

Not very long after the University opened its doors the Trustees invited its members to an evening reception in Cobb Hall, at that time the only academic building erected. Very attractively decorated tables were provided for the refreshments; but after the party was over, it was discovered that not only forks and spoons but the handsome maroon ribbons which had been used to trim the tables had been stripped off and carried away. The question was how to bring to the attention of the community that such hoodlumism was not to be counted among the social customs which were to prevail. Fortunately, it was not difficult to get unofficial expressions of condemnation of such acts, but it was a long time before similar depradations wholly ceased. It was not uncommon when receptions or parties were held in the Women's Halls for the guests to carry off pieces of bric-a-brac from the public rooms, and even personal articles from the students' rooms, which had to be used as coat rooms.

Early in the first winter President and Mrs. Harper gave a delightful evening party, for which they issued very handsome engraved invitations. There was some curiosity as to where this work was done, for engraving for social functions was not commonly practiced in Chicago. One of the guests at the party, a professor in the University, appeared in his customary slouchy and well-worn working suit of clothes and was heard to inquire of the President why he had not let him know what kind of a party it was to be! To the group as a whole the form of the invitation gave sufficient information.

One day in the early winter two women students came to me in evident perplexity. One of them said that a man student had stopped her on the stairway in Cobb Hall and asked her if she would go with him to a dance some of the men were arranging to give a few days later at a public hall in the neighborhood. She had come from a community where it was customary for private parties to be given and gentlemen to be invited as guests; so she was in doubt as to whether to accept and had postponed her reply. The other woman received a similar invitation, but her "hold-up" was on the street. My previous experience gave me no ready answer. I said, "Let us find out how parties are given and invitations issued by the people who are showing interest in the University." I said, "I have no inclination to force on the community the standards to which I have been accustomed, but I do not think we are compelled to adopt the standards of Podunk." I went out to make inquiries, knowing well what I should learn and knowing that, if we followed the local customs of which I learned, we should do just about what was observed the world around in the best society. I finally advised (a mild term!) that the undergraduates should not go to the party and that the graduates might do as they pleased. I confess that this was not kind. The graduates had much discussion among themselves. Several declined their invitations; but a few accepted and had a miserable evening, for it was known by that time that a social *faux pas* had been made. The papers got hold of the incident and made up a story of how the undergraduate women, compelled by the Dean to remain housed, flattened their noses against the window panes of the Hotel Beatrice and enviously watched the more fortunate merrymakers pass by. This so misrepresented the students' attitude, for we had all agreed as to the proper procedure, that a delegation waited on President Harper to assure him that the story absolutely misrepresented the facts. Two weeks later a large party was organized along most respectable and approved lines. There was a large attendance, and "an enjoyable evening was had by all." A red-headed youth, who had called on me in quite a rage to protest against the decision in regard to the first party, called again some weeks later. He told me that on the occasion of his previous call he had left determined never to enter the building again, he felt so enraged. Evidently his red hair did not indicate long-lasting bad temper, for he wished me to know that, on thinking the matter over, he was very glad, in case he had a sister who wanted to enter the University, to know that some degree of social protection would be given her and social standards set before her.

Another case will help show how interesting and important it was to establish social influences which would aid in strengthening the position of the new University in the academic world. At a private dinner which Mrs. Palmer attended before the University opened, the plans for the advancement of scholarship were set forth to a group of prominent citizens. When reference was casually made to women as members of the University, somebody exclaimed, "How can the University be the dignified body of scholars you intend it to be if women are to be included!" This reaction to the generous and farsighted plans of the Founder and the President reinforced the determination Mrs. Palmer and I had already made that the presence of women should never mean the lowering of any standards, intellectual or social. From the outset the women students gave their active and sympathetic support to this resolution.

Social standards and customs change so greatly from generation to generation that it is often difficult to appreciate the significance of an event which occurred forty or fifty years previously. It would certainly not be easy, even if it were possible, for a young graduate student in 1930, in the age of hip flasks and bootlegging, to comprehend the stir made by an incident which occurred at the Hotel Beatrice early in January, 1893; but the group at that time was convinced that a crisis was at hand.

The dining-rooms of the Beatrice accommodated, in addition to the regular residents, several women students who had rooms in the neighborhood. One day two graduate students came to me in some distress and said they found themselves in a trying position and wondered if I could help them out of it. One of the women fellows had had a dinner party during the holidays and told these students that she had some wine left and would like to invite some friends to "drink it up." Her room, however, was not a suitable place in which to entertain guests, and she asked the privilege of using the room occupied by these students. They were taken aback, but were at a loss as to how to refuse the request. The fellow then proceeded to invite guests. One after another accepted, though most of them with some qualms. Drinking, especially by women, was in those days not often made the sole feature of a social gathering. Indeed, drinking at all was practically taboo among women in academic circles. It chanced that the hostess gave her invitation, in the presence of other students, to one of the most admired and outstanding young scholars of the new community, who forthwith declined. The word passed quickly from one to another that Helen Tunnicliff had refused her invitation. She was so greatly admired that doubts arose at once. Immediately the doubts were crystallized into certainty, and all the women involved as guests were eager to be released from the party. "Of course," was my reply, "it surely cannot be that a group of graduate women in the new University, who are already under rather severe inspection and criticism, will gather for the sole purpose of drinking. I will see Miss ---------, and you may consider yourselves free from your pledge." I thought the interview would be easy; but when she entered the room, an imposing figure of some 175 pounds with height to correspond, I felt that my 93 pounds and short stature were at a disadvantage and that the strength of our determination would have to prove in inverse ratio to our size. When I told her that I thought it might prove very damaging to the University and the status of women scholars if it should be known that such a gathering as she proposed were to take place and that I would like to have her help avoid such an outcome by recalling her invitations, she became very angry and said she had had wide experience in educational institutions and never had experienced such interference with personal liberty. I replied that the use of wine was not what I objected to, for I had been used to seeing it served on social occasions such as dinners, and that if the graduate women were to gather to hear a paper read or meet a distinguished scholar, no one could make up a discreditable story if a glass of wine were passed with other refreshments. The gathering for the sole purpose of "drinking up" wine left over from another function was quite a different matter and could not be allowed. She asked by what authority I thought I could stop it. I replied, "By the authority of the Dean of Women, responsible for the good name of the women of the University." She then said that German professors drank at their meetings, to which comment I replied that we were "talking about American ladies, not German professors," and that my decision must be considered final. It was with a sigh of relief that the proposed guests heard what the outcome of our conference was, but none of them fully realized how grateful I was for being informed of the plan in time to avoid the hazard which was involved.

The changes time has wrought make it difficult to realize that even in the latter part of the nineteenth century many religious sects were still very strict in regard to social amusements. Theater-going, card-playing, and dancing were diversions calling for church discipline. It was difficult for those of us who were used to greater freedom to realize how distinctly the University was a Baptist institution, the President and a majority of the Trustees required by the charter to be Baptists. Courtesy and policy alike demanded consideration for their views, although no regulations embodying the restrictions observed generally by Baptists had been laid down by the Trustees. It was agreed quite early by the residents of the Women's Halls that there should be no card-playing in the public rooms, and consequently none at parties where men were guests. Dancing could not be made so private an affair, and almost at once it became the custom for the women students to dance together for a little while after dinner in the large social rooms where there were pianos. Evidently news of this got bruited about, as well as rumors of projected dances for men and women. It was startling to have the matter brought up at a meeting of the University Council and to have the Dean of the Divinity School make a motion that no dancing should be permitted in any University building. Fright is a mild term to apply to my reaction. I was still enough of a Puritan to have a horror of public dance halls; and yet those were the places to which students, men and women alike, who had no objection to dancing would have to resort, and the probability was that under the influence of the prohibition they would dance in season and out of season and much more frequently than they would actually desire. I summoned all my courage and described to the Council the situation as I saw it. I must have presented an impressive picture of the evils likely to attend the patronage of public places of amusement and the utter inability of the University to protect itself and its members from possible harm. I then moved that student organizations should hold no dances *except* in University buildings. My arguments had been so effective that the motion was passed and remained in force for several years. Gradually, however, the rule was relaxed. Parties could be held in private houses, but even then under general regulations laid down by the Board of Student Organizations. Slowly, very slowly, a list of approved hotels and public halls was established. Their managers were eager for the patronage and seldom showed any reluctance to conform to the wishes of the University, fearing lest approval might be withdrawn. From hotels in the neighborhood the list grew; and the first large formal dance given in a leading downtown hotel created much excitement. Permission was withdrawn from a large and select social clubhouse because of the use of liquor contrary to agreement.

Such are some of the happenings at a time when the social standards of the new institution were taking form. The University was in the limelight because of its many adventurous and radical plans; and there were plenty of critics ready to ridicule, if not to condemn ruthlessly, its various activities. Those who believed that the University had a big contribution to make toward fine scholarship had to be constantly on their guard lest some slight misstep might harm the whole undertaking. It was very remarkable how clearly the women of the University, older and younger, understood this and how loyally and intelligently they co-operated in every measure that was undertaken to strengthen their position as important factors in the success of the enterprise.

CHAPTER FIVE

Kindred Spirits

One day a student was registering a social affair in my office and I said to him, "You don't seem very interested or enthusiastic."

"No," he replied, "I don't see much sense in having the party."

"Why, then, do you have it?" I asked.

"It's the tradition," was his reply.

"How long has it been the tradition?" was my next question.

"Oh, ever since I have been in the University."

"How long is that?"

"Two years."

"Well," I said, "the first time that party was given was the second year before you came. Charles Lamb wrote of 'the marrow of tradition.' If this tradition has no marrow it is no good; put a stop to it, here and now. Don't be afraid."

There is a rather widespread opinion that youth are fearless and radical. This may be true in some directions, but in my experience they are almost invariably ultraconservative in social matters. They are servants, not masters, of their social customs. They ape, they do not initiate, both individually and in groups. For this reason the student body has often been unsuccessful in attempts to reorganize or disband societies or clubs which have outlived their purpose or proved objectionable. Several times attempts were made to abolish women's secret clubs. Courageous and quite intelligent efforts to limit the number of official positions one person could hold (the point system) always proved futile. At intervals the great multiplicity of organizations and the consequent overlapping of functions (if such a serious term could be applied) have led to a demand for simplicity, even to the point of abolishing all and starting fresh. Sometimes the only result has been that the mountain has brought forth a mouse, another feeble organization for the same rather limited group of so-called leading students to officer. There seems to be an almost awesome respect for what is and a hesitancy about replacing it by what should be. And yet anemia is often fatal, especially pernicious anemia; and there has been a high rate of mortality in the organizations. It might be thought that the University should step in and give the coup de grâce, but its policy has been to allow any group of students to organize, provided they stated their purpose and conformed to the simple rules laid down by the University. A study of the organizations which, month after month, have been given approval by the authorities would be richer in amount and more significant in content than is sometimes the case in Master's theses. If there had been no mortality, if little groups had not quietly expired, the University would have been in a sad plight. The condition has been bad enough in any case.

On the whole, the women's organizations have steered clear of serious difficulties, especially those groups which included a large number of women. Many, many little groups have been formed and given much pleasure and quietly lapsed. For several years after the University was opened, no need was felt for any general organization of the women; but in 1901 the Board of Student Organizations authorized a commission under the chairmanship of the Dean of Women to proceed to the formation of a woman's club. On December 19 a constitution was adopted, and the Woman's Union of the University of Chicago started out on its useful and interesting career. All women connected with the University were eligible to membership on the payment of a quarterly fee of fifty cents or an annual fee of one dollar. The object was to unite the women of the University for the promotion of their common interests. The Disciples Church, a quaint, oddly shaped little building at the corner of Fifty-seventh Street and what was then called Lexington Avenue, was obtained for the use of the Union on weekdays, and the rooms were formally opened on January 8, 1902. There were not only accommodations for assemblies of considerable size; but in addition provision was made for a restroom, a reading-room, and a lunchroom. Receptions and entertainments were given weekly, and many distinguished women were the guests of the Union. Under the skilful direction of Miss Susan Wade Peabody, luncheons were prepared and served by the students; and twice a week music was provided at the luncheon hour by a student committee. By special arrangement the secretary of the Young Women's Christian Association, or, as it was called for a time, the Women Students' Christian League, held daily office hours at the rooms; and other organizations of students occasionally had the use of the rooms for their functions. Much hard work was put into managing and carrying out the details of the undertaking, and a fine spirit of co-operation and service was developed. The experience in meeting responsibility was a valuable one. In addition, the happy companionship and the not infrequent merrymakings joined in making a store of very precious memories for all who participated, students and Faculty women alike.

The same general procedure was followed when in 1902, on the sudden and surprising erection of Lexington Hall, the church was returned to its rapidly growing membership and new quarters in the women's building were occupied. The lunchroom administration was transferred to the Women's Commons. This greatly lightened the labor and responsibility of the members of the Union, but also resulted in losses of various kinds, especially in intimate social contacts and opportunities for certain types of initiative.

As time went on, it became apparent that voluntary and more or less casual services were no longer adequate, especially in view of the increasing number of women in the University and the demands made upon them. Keeping up the membership list and collecting fees was an exacting task. Quarterly tickets of different colors had to be issued four times a year; and the officers, if not the members, were often reminded of the popular lines written at the time that different-colored slips were issued on the street cars depending on the amount of the fare which had to be paid:

A pink trip slip for a six-cent fare.
A green trip slip for an eight-cent fare, and so on.
    Punch in the presence of the passengare.

A regularly employed executive officer seemed necessary, but no funds were available. It was therefore decided to disband and proceed to the formation of a different type of organization. This action was precipitated by a communication sent on June 27, 1914, to the Board of Student Organizations by a committee of Spelman House (the one non-residential house which had been established), whose chairman was Ethel Preston. This committee suggested that a new organization be formed to consist of representatives of all organizations which had women members, together with the faculty women of the Colleges of Arts, Literature, and Science, and a representative from the Faculty of the College of Education. The purposes of this council were to be the supervision of the social life of the University women, the formation of a well-balanced social calendar, and the development of plans for the administration of Ida Noyes Hall.

The provisions for membership in the Woman's Administrative Council, as adopted in the first constitution, were as follows:

1. Representatives of organizations made up exclusively of women and which are social in character
2. The University aides
3. The Senior women on the Student Council
4. Three members at large chosen by the Council

5. The Dean of Women

6. The Director of Physical Education

7. A member of the Faculty of the College of Education chosen by the Council

8. A member of the Faculty of Arts, Literature, and Science chosen by the Council

The Executive Head, or a member of an associated organization, shall be its representative on the Council.

Additions to the membership may be made by the Council upon recommendation by the Executive Committee.

The following is a list of the original members:

Marion Talbot	Dean of Women
Gertrude Dudley	Director of Physical Education for Women
Gertrude Van Hoesen	Faculty of the College of Education
Elizabeth Wallace	Faculty of Arts, Literature, and Science
Julia Dodge	Young Women's Christian League
Alma Parmele	Woman's Athletic Association
Elsie Johns	Neighborhood Clubs
Agnes Riddell	Women's Graduate Club
Dorothy Strachan	Women's Glee Club
Marie Goodenough	Inter-Club Council
Emma Low	Spelman House
Leona Coons	Nancy Foster Hall
Pauline Levi	Green Hall
Ruth Wiesinger	Kelly Hall
Ethel Mott	Greenwood Hall
Florence Bradley	Beecher Hall
Treva Mathews	Masquers
Ruth Allen	Student Council
Katherine Biggins	University aide

Caryl Cody	University aide
Katherine Covert	University aide
Phyllis Fay	University aide
Grace Hotchkiss	University aide
Hilda MacClintock	University aide
Mary MacDonald	University aide
Edith Smith	University aide
Irene Tufts	University aide
Ruth Allen	University aide
Jeannette Harvey	Harpischord

Changes in the constitution were made later, partly in the make-up of the membership and, of greater importance, in making the promotion of the common interests (not merely the social life) of the women of the University the purpose of the Council. One of the original provisions was that an undergraduate student should be president. The result of this was that no interest was shown by the graduate women. This condition was remedied when the purpose was broadened and less emphasis was placed on undergraduate interests as such.

Under the presidency of Katherine Biggins the new organization started out on what proved to be a rather brief but important career. It was not long before the women's dream of a special building for their activities was realized through the generous gift of Mr. LaVerne Noyes, and all the interests of Ida Noyes Hall were placed in the hands of a special commission appointed by President Judson. Then came the World War with its absorbing interests and the Woman Students' Training Corps, which, on the termination of the war, was reorganized as the Federation of University Women. Thereupon it was decided by the Women's Administrative Council to suspend operations until such time as its larger object of promoting the interests of all the women of the University, and not merely the undergraduates, could be served without duplication of effort.

One undertaking of the Council is worth noting in some detail, because it threw light on some questions which had been raised as to how the social life could be enriched and made to reach the women who in large numbers, it was asserted, had no social contacts and who felt the University to be a cold and unfriendly community. It was decided to have a general "social rally" on February 24, 1915, with refreshments and various forms of entertainment, and to send personal invitations to women undergraduates not enrolled as members of student organizations. Special committees were formed to carry out the plan, and a large number of the most prominent and socially experienced students devoted considerable time and effort to the attempt to solve what seemed to be a serious defect in the University life. Special pains were taken not to make known the basis on which invitations were sent. The outcome was that of the 239 invited, 19 were present! The total number present was 57, and this meant that there were twice as many hostesses as guests. Seven accepted in advance but were not present, and 11 sent regrets. No response was heard from 221. It was a disheartened and disappointed group that pondered the situation after the party was over. A generous and altruistic spirit had had a bad shock. Cynicism threatened to take its place. We all had to remind ourselves that in a group whose homes were in large measure in the city, other social ties and home obligations would doubtless be too absorbing to make social life in the University a factor in the students' lives. A view which I had always held was, to my regret, confirmed. My experience in the past had often led me to believe that some individuals seem obsessed with the idea that the world's hand is against them, and no matter how often kindly and gracious social overtures may be made to them, the only reaction is that they withdraw still farther into their shells. Of course, one may be expected to go halfway in a gesture of friendliness; but going all the way and even then not meeting with any response is rather discouraging. In time it leads to a certain degree of cynicism and a willingness to let people "enjoy being left out," to paraphrase the old woman's phrase that she was "enjoying poor health, thank you." We came to the conclusion, some of us, that people of this type should be left to take the few steps needed to put themselves in touch with the different social activities which were announced as open to all, and not be coerced into social relationships against their will and at considerable cost to their well-wishers. Another and very different group consists of those who are inherently timid but who respond, though perhaps shyly, to expressions of friendliness. Any community made up, as the University is, of young people—not the young only—with different kinds of social background must have leadership which takes this situation into account and tries to solve the difficulties it presents. It is clear that the precept "Children should be seen and not heard" dominates in many—not all, indeed—American homes. While in some groups the children occupy the whole of the scene, in others they are nonentities; in very few are they taught the art of conversation. In a survey which Miss Breckinridge and I made of the women in the Junior Colleges the response we received as to what they most wished to gain from their college was almost invariably in one form or another "to be at ease in social situations." I have no doubt that many of the Faculty families also, who tried to show hospitality to students, would have been glad if this could have been accomplished, for it was not easy to entertain shy and speechless guests. It is dangerous to generalize from such experiences as the Sunday-night supper to which a much-loved dean invited about one hundred students, of whom six appeared; or from the jolly class parties which Professor Miller gave at his home; or from the stone walls of men at class dances, who were adamant in refusing to be introduced to women whose appearance did not suit them; or, from the amazingly beautiful and popular Senior woman, Suzanne Haskell, declining all invitations to dance with attractive and eager young men "socialites" of the University, and, as one of the hostesses at a dance given by the Woman's Union, selecting as her partners one after another of the shy, awkward, and admiring lads who were in the social background.

A long story could be made of the varied groupings of students, and it would often awaken happy memories; but the story would be too long. One group, however, must not be passed by—the Club of Women Fellows. It was organized after an experiment by President Harper in devising a method by which the graduate students could gain experience in conducting the affairs of a college faculty. He realized, as I often had occasion to point out to women graduate students, that pure specialization in a field of scholarship usually has to be supplemented with a knowledge both of the significance of other subjects in an educational program and of practical and efficient methods of administering such a program. Accordingly, when, under pressure of work, he had to relinquish the direction of his "little faculty," the time seemed ripe to call together the women Fellows, since it seemed probable that they would soon be called upon to take some responsibility in conducting the affairs of schools, if not of colleges. Monthly meetings were held in Kelly Hall or Green Hall; and after luncheon, sitting in a large circle—for we numbered from twelve to twenty—each one told of the investigation she was carrying on and discussed general problems of education. On one occasion I invited Mrs. Potter Palmer, who was generally acknowledged to be the leader of Chicago society, to be a guest of the Club. Mrs. Palmer was a woman of wide experience in affairs of the world, not only in this country but in Europe. It was quite clear, however, that she had never had an experience like this one; and she was very enthusiastic about having had the opportunity to meet the young scholars and to learn from them personally about their research.

A different type of organization needs some consideration. As has been related, President Harper, in opening the first meeting of the Faculty of Arts, Literature, and Science on October I, 1892, after a few general remarks, outlined some specific topics for consideration. The first of these was the establishment of secret societies. The subject had been considered already by the Board of Trustees, who suggested various restrictions. A chapter of a fraternity had been organized, and this fact precipitated a controversy which continued in various aspects through the succeeding years. It was clearly intended that the term "secret societies" meant fraternities, not sororities. A large number of the Faculty, probably a majority, were opposed to having the system introduced and were distinctly offended by having it thrust down their throats. Action was delayed so that a special committee might consider the matter and present recommendations. It followed that approval was given with unwonted restrictions. It was not long before there were signs that some of the national sororities were taking steps to establish chapters. Mrs. Palmer and I made it known that we were familiar with both the advantages and disadvantages of this type of social organization and that, at least during the formative period of the University, we would oppose its introduction. We realized that in many institutions sororities afforded housing and social life which otherwise would not be available for women students. As the University of Chicago was to provide both these essential factors in the life of its students, and in addition the city provided cultural and social opportunities usually not within the reach of students in a small town, it seemed to us important that the situation should not be complicated by the introduction of policies directed by persons outside of the University and not familiar with its aims. As a result no further steps were taken at the time.

In 1894 Mrs. Palmer and I had a conference with three brilliant and able women undergraduates—Agnes Cook, Eleanor Jones, and Helen Thompson—who asked approval of a plan for the formation of a club for literary and social purposes. Although the element of secrecy was not very apparent, the basis of membership was highly selective; and we both felt considerable apprehension lest a factor be introduced into the life of the women which would be at variance with our plans. The high character of these students, their evident seriousness, and their worthy aims carried the day, although we realized that any pledges they eagerly made could not be binding on future generations. I wrote as follows to President Harper:

> I trust that you are pleased with the proposed women's undergraduate society, and that you approve of the dignified and self-respecting way in which they have made known the formation of their organization. It is the outcome of another struggle on the fraternity question which, though hydra-headed, has thus far been kept under control. I believe that this society will be a help in meeting the efforts of secret societies which are ambitious and eager to found chapters in our University, even against the judgment of our best and strongest women. If you approve of this movement, I trust there may be a chance for you to tell the young women who are concerned in it; if you have any suggestions to make, I am sure they will gladly receive them, as they have the interests of the University as much at heart as their own personal pleasure.

He returned the letter with the following comment: "Very much indeed. Please secure me the chance to express my feelings."

Following their example, four other groups took similar steps. The club system was established, and soon the features which we had dreaded appeared. For years, and even now, as with the fraternities, discussion has been continuous, criticism and defense have been keen, and at intervals there have been sharp controversies. Naturally, the national sororities have wished to extend their influence, and probably their prestige, by having chapters in the University of Chicago. The first clubs were hardly on their feet before rumors were rife that in fact and in secret they were chapters of sororities. This was officially denied by their respective presidents, who emphatically repudiated misstatements made in the Chicago papers and even in the *University of Chicago Weekly.*

In 1896 steps were taken by outside women to establish a chapter of a sorority. At that time I sent the following letter to President Harper:

> When Mrs. Palmer and I undertook to organize and influence the life and activities of the women of the University, we agreed to try to establish three principles—liberty, equality, unity. In view of the special conditions which distinguish this University from all others to which women are admitted, we thought that we could be successful in securing these characteristics to a degree entirely unknown elsewhere.
>
> Although Mrs. Palmer was a member of a fraternity, she believed that methods of this kind of organization were in distinct antagonism to the ends we were seeking; and we both agreed that even though in some colleges these societies might offer some advantages, together with their generally acknowledged disadvantages, we should discourage every effort to establish them here, where the spirit of a great University, rather than of a provincial college, should be fostered. Since the general vote of the Trustees allowing fraternities to be established was passed without special reference to the effect on the somewhat complicated and extremely important form of house organization which was developing among the women, we have acted in accordance with our own judgment; and when, from time to time, women from other institutions have visited us with a view to establishing their fraternities here, we have told them of our preferences and they have courteously withdrawn.
>
> Believing that it was very desirable that we should not seek to maintain a policy which should be at variance with the spirit of the University, I have, on every possible occasion, sought to learn the real preference of the students. The fact that for nearly four years no organization was formed, although there had been no prohibition and no general knowledge or discussion of our position, has led me to think that there was no demand for fraternities on the part of our women.

In March, 1896, steps were taken by women from other institutions to establish a chapter here. When I learned of this, I
decided that possibly my own views should be modified; and I
stood ready to do this and always shall on any subject when, with
further knowledge, I am convinced that it should be done. At the
same time I made up my mind that no system involving the social relations of all the women of the University could be justly
introduced without the approval of those who were even only
indirectly involved. As the first step in securing the information
I needed, I called a meeting of the women officers of the University. Of the twenty-six invited, twenty-two came and, greatly to my
surprise, voted *unanimously* and signed a paper to the effect that in
their opinion the establishment of sororities in this University is
undesirable. Several of those who thus voted were active and loyal
members of sororities in other places. They appointed a committee to ask the women of the University Colleges to consider the
subject. The meeting which was called was not largely attended,
probably because of the near approach of the examinations; but of
those who voted, three-quarters were opposed to having fraternities here. . . .

In view of the fact that a petition has been received from a few
women asking for the recognition of a society which, if granted,
will be followed by the enforced establishment of the whole system, and in view also of the desire of many of the women who
have responsibility and influence that the system should not
be introduced during this formative period, will it not be possible
for you to call together the women of the Senior Colleges and ask
for an expression of their opinion as to whether fraternities should
be established now or postponed until some later time when
there should be a general demand for them from within rather than
without?

I realize fully that the simplest and easiest way of solving the
problem would be to recognize the fraternities at once; but though
the dangers which I foresee and which the older women in other

institutions warn us against will not come in large measure until after I give up my charge, I am ready to do all in my power and spare no effort to establish the life of the women here upon lines along which it can permanently develop to the highest good of the institution and its members.

The women officers sent in the following communication:

At a meeting of the women officers, including fellows, held on March 20, 1896, at which twenty-two out of twenty-six were present, the following resolution was unanimously adopted:

Resolved: That it is the sense of this meeting that under the conditions existing in this University it is not advisable to introduce sororities.

Some of the arguments leading to this resolution were:

1. Since the local chapter is governed by the general organization, the presence of sororities here would mean a certain degree of influence upon our government by other institutions.

2. It is the policy of this University to emphasize a democratic spirit by means of the house life, and it is felt that sororities would militate against this policy.

3. In our University, in the midst of this large city, there are already too many distractions and demands upon the time of the students without the additional demands arising from sororities.

A committee was then appointed which was empowered to call a meeting of the women of the University Colleges to lay before them this resolution and to ascertain their opinion on the subject.

It was perhaps natural that a poll of the members of the women's clubs resulted in an expression of their desire that sororities should not enter the University. This, theoretically at least, put an end to the rumors that the clubs were actually *sub rosa* chapters of sororities.

A vigorous and not altogether satisfactory correspondence was carried on with those who were most active in pushing the proposed chapter. The interest of certain influential women had been secured; but when they learned of the prevailing opposition among the women of the University, they withdrew their support. Considerable time was thus spent. In the course of the discussion the request was brought officially to the Board of Student Organizations. A special committee was appointed on March 20, 1897, to consider the matter further.

REPORT OF SPECIAL COMMITTEE OF THE BOARD OF STUDENT ORGANIZATIONS APPOINTED TO CONSIDER THE APPLICATION OF ALICE PEIRCE AND OTHERS TO ESTABLISH A CHAPTER OF PI BETA PHI FRATERNITY

Your Committee would report that, of the seven petitioners, three have left the University and two have withdrawn their names from the petition. Two of the patronesses, Miss Helen Culver and Mrs. W. I. Thomas, have declined to serve and have expressed their regret that they did not earlier understand the full significance of the project.

Your Committee would recommend (1) that the request be laid upon the table; (2) that no similar requests be granted until some of the problems now engrossing the attention of the women be more nearly solved and until it be evident that there is a general demand for the fraternity system from a considerable body of the students, indorsed by the women of the Faculty; (3) that the present request, together with those already informally received by Miss Talbot, receive the first attention if in the future the system should be introduced.

In June, 1897, the following action was taken by the Board:

1. That the petitioners be notified that the Council does not deem it expedient to grant their request; and

2. That no similar requests be granted until some of the problems now engrossing the attention of the women be more nearly solved, and until it be evident that there is a general demand for the fraternity system from a considerable body of the students, indorsed by the women of the Faculty.

3. That the present request, together with those already informally received by Dean Talbot, receive the first attention if in the future the system should be introduced.

This action showed that, although Mrs. Palmer's official connection with the University had ended two years previously, her convictions were shared by many of the Faculty.

Nevertheless, the question would not down. To a great many persons, even to members of the University, the situation seemed to mean discrimination against women. Accordingly, in June, 1897, the following communication was received by me:

The following communication of the University Council to the Board of Student Organizations, etc., was received by the Board of Student Organizations, etc., and adopted, and the reference voted, at its meeting of June 5, 1897:

The Council requests the Board of Student Organizations, etc., to refer to the women officers for further consideration the question of the introduction of women fraternities and their adaptation to the house life among the women.

It was also voted that the women officers be requested to report on this and similar matters referred to it at the December meeting of the Board.

It was a considerable time before the matter reached the Board of Student Organizations and could be referred to the women as directed. Their reply follows:

Two questions were submitted by the Board to the women officers
of the University, viz.:

I. The further consideration of the introduction of women's
intercollegiate fraternities and their adaptation to the house life
among the women.

II. The withdrawal of approval from all secret local clubs among
the women and the forbidding of the initiation of women students
into these clubs.

The questions were first submitted by the Dean of Women to
the Club of Women Fellows. After prolonged discussion it was declared by a vote of 13 to 0, 1 not voting, to be the judgment of the
Club that intercollegiate fraternities are not at present adapted to
the life of the women of the University of Chicago.

At a subsequent meeting it was unanimously voted that in the
opinion of the Club of Women Fellows approval should not at present be withdrawn from the local secret clubs, although the Club
considers them as strictly experimental and therefore urges the
Board of Student Organizations to encourage all forms of association which tend to promote a spirit of unity and democracy and
to develop those qualities which result from co-operative effort.

The action taken by the Club was heartily indorsed by the wom-
en of the Faculty, and the Dean therefore begs leave to submit that
both questions are answered in the negative by the women officers.

The years passed uneventfully after these decisions had been
reached, except for occasional inquiries as to the attitude of the
University in regard to sororities, until 1924. At that time Dean
Ernest H. Wilkins organized a campaign among the students for
a "Better Yet Chicago." Among the committees he organized was
one to consider the introduction of sororities. Rather reluctantly I assume he was not aware he was taking on a responsibility
which, if not solely mine, was ours jointly, for he neither consulted me as to my views nor made known his plan to me until it

was publicly announced. Many meetings and much talk ensued, but after a great to-do the subject again disappeared from the arena of public and official discussion. On my retirement in 1925, it was commonly believed and openly stated that "now that Dean Talbot has retired, the sororities will come in." But the anticipated invasion did not take place. Adverse opinion had grown rather than weakened; and the future of the men's fraternities, which was beginning to look dubious, added to the prevailing reluctance to complicate the problem by the presence of sororities.

Meanwhile, what of the clubs? As Mrs. Palmer and I dreaded, they rapidly lost their original characteristics and assumed the traits of sororities, with one exception, which seemed to us extremely important, viz., no outside organization had any voice in their management and the University could at any time eliminate or modify them without difficult complications. Anyone going over the happenings and the discussions of the years which have elapsed would find in them ample material for an *opera bouffe*. Criticisms and difficulties arose thick and fast. In spite of the rulings of the University that no student could be initiated into a secret society whose work was not of passing grade, names of proposed initiates were often presented to me to be ruled upon who were found to be on probation. "Rushing," so-called, became an evil which it was sought to overcome by sets of rules, sometimes so minute as to be ridiculous and always such as to interfere with normal, friendly relations between older and younger students. Interclub councils, graduate advisory councils, and committees galore passed regulations, rescinded them, made new ones, again reverted to the original ones; and meanwhile faculty committees worked on the problem of how to make the clubs capable of exercising their genuine merits and at the same time doing away with trivial and envy- and suspicion-breeding practices. At one time the opposition to the system was so strong that some of the ablest and most prominent women students withdrew in protest from their clubs. It was hoped that this action might result in abolishing them; but many influences, some sentimental, some practical, were too strong. From time to time there have been great improvements in their methods, and the Faculty have never cared to carry their doubts to the point of ruling against their continuance. Undoubtedly, some students have greatly profited by them and had social pleasures which would not otherwise have been within their reach; but, as I have seen the situation, this advantage has been far more than offset by the disappointments and ill feeling which have been caused among other students. Their significance in the social life of the University has been ridiculously overestimated. The number of members has always been comparatively small but rather conspicuous. Those students who have found social activity in connection with department clubs, religious organizations, the Athletic Association, the Young Women's Christian Association, the classes, and the many other organizations which the University has fostered, have enjoyed friendly associations more in keeping with the interests of intellectual, than of high social life.

CHAPTER SIX

New Homes for Old

At the time the University was organized, women were just beginning to feel the shackles loosen which had been fettering them. The recently established women's colleges were showing signs of revolt. The confiscation of the score of a Gilbert and Sullivan opera or the refusal of a request to see Edwin Booth act in Hamlet were typical illustrations of the kind of discipline which could not fetter much longer the eager and adventurous young spirits who had chosen the pioneers' pathway to higher scholarship. To the world in general, and the college world in particular, the situation was confusing. No formulation of the principles which should guide the new freedom had been worked out to take the place of the old restrictions and taboos. That was the first problem Mrs. Palmer and I had to solve. When I expressed my doubt as to whether I had had sufficient experience to justify my undertaking the new responsibilities and duties of the deanship, Mrs. Palmer said quite simply, "All that you need to remember is that you will be an older student among younger ones and an older woman with more experience among younger ones eager to learn." Mrs. Palmer sounded the keynote for the new life. The organization and conduct of the Women's Houses of the new University, as well as the social life in general of the University, should be based on principles of unity, liberty, and social responsibility. Certain phases of these principles I later worked out more in detail.

The practical application of these principles began at once.

*Students at Hotel Beatrice, October 1, 1892: Margaret Purcell, Elizabeth Butler,
Cora Roche, Grace Clark, Demia Butler*

No time was to be lost; no conflicting event could be allowed to
pass unnoticed lest it crystallize into a fixed attitude or custom
and pass beyond the reach of suggestion or influence.

The practice field was immediately available. The Hotel Beatrice, an unfinished, six-story "flat building" bearing the words
"World Fair Rooms To Let" painted high up on its outside wall,
with a small two-story annex; placed in a section of Chicago in
transition from country to city, with here and there the marks
of once prosperous farms and buildings boldly attempting to be
strictly urban in architecture; neighboring streets not yet paved,
sidewalks for the most part merely plank walks—this was the
first, and fortunately temporary, home of the University women
which Mrs. Palmer and I found the morning after our arrival.
Even though long months had been given to preliminary preparations, the University did not open its doors with provision for
every contingency, especially the housing.

Essential articles of bedroom furniture had been ordered and were beginning to arrive—beds, mattresses, chairs—but evidently the "amenities were to wait," as Virginia Woolf, in *A Room of One's Own*, said was the case in the women's colleges of England. Our decision was immediate that the wait must not be long. An environment of comfort and of as much beauty as possible was essential to our plan. Fortunately, Mrs. Martin A. Ryerson and Mrs. Charles L. Hutchinson, with their special interest in the University through their husbands and with their exquisite taste, came to the rescue and chose modest but attractive draperies and pieces of furniture for my living-room and the two tiny rooms to be used for social purposes. But there were the piles of mattresses to be distributed and frames of bedsteads to be put together and, even so, not enough to accommodate all the students who were piling in on us, to say nothing of the members of the Faculty and their families who were to make their temporary homes under our roof. The challenge of the professor in the Divinity School that his bed springs had to be taken up to the sixth floor was met in his absence by some plucky American girls. Another head professor, Mr. Laughlin, a man of sensitive spirit and known as a stickler for good form, seeing them struggling with their load, lent a hand, thinking he was securing a good night's rest for some woman student. His dismay, when he discovered that he was doing a porter's work for a huskier man than himself, well repaid the girls for their part in the incident. Then there was the distinguished professor from England who put his "boots" outside his bedroom door to be cleaned, not realizing that the establishment was as yet without a single "menial." The same adventurous young members of the University saw to it that he was not disappointed, and he never suspected how it happened! And he had to be given help when he asked where he could get some "spirits"—not meaning the high kind that was about him on every side, but something with which he could "brew a cup." It was incidents like these that kept our spirits up and that made the close

of the day—perhaps an hour well into the night—when Mrs.
Palmer and I met after our various academic, domestic, and social
duties and prepared ourselves for our well-earned slumbers, a
time of genuine recreation. We would recount to each other what
had been our experiences, and be convulsed with laughter as we
realized the humor of the situation in which we found ourselves.
I really believe we could not have done our day's work if it had
not been for these periods of hilarity.

When we discovered that the lighting fixtures had not been put
in, another friend came to our rescue. Dean Harry Pratt Judson
produced some candles and beer bottles in a manner so friendly
and winsome that we made no inquiries as to their source. After
a couple of days of picnicking and generally "roughing it" in the
matter of food, he took a large party of us to the Hyde Park Hotel
for dinner. I think china and glass never seemed so shiny, or linen
whiter, or black waiters so magnificent, as they did to us after our
short taste of life removed from civilization.

As no arrangements had been made for a housekeeper, or even
a cook, that was another matter for immediate attack. The business authorities of the University seemed somewhat surprised
when the two deans said they could not do the work, especially
when one of them was in Cambridge; and in a few days we had
both helpers installed. Meanwhile, Mrs. Palmer and I got together some breakfasts very much in the way that boys camping out
often do, scrambled eggs proving the staple dish. This menu was
in part due to the almost complete lack of kitchen equipment, for
we were really quite skilled cooks. But the cook who came proved
a will-o'-the-wisp, not always on the job in the morning or even at
dinner time. When we remonstrated, he said, "Ladies, you see it
is this way. I have a girl; and when it is a choice between love and
dooty, love wins." We soon had a successor who was free from
such an encumbrance.

But even a cook could not attend to all the details of providing for a family of sixty, with thirty more coming in from outside

quarters. Again the Business Department came to our relief and sent word that they had found an exceptionally skilled man who could not only do the buying and keep the accounts but would see that nice touches were put on the dining-room service. Mrs. Palmer and I were asked to interview him and tell him our wishes. After a conference, which left us with the belief that we must at least give the man a trial, Mr. Benbow turned, on leaving the room, and said, "Oh, ladies! There is one point I forgot—would you prefer to have the toothpicks on the different tables or on a stand by the door?" It is needless to say that his reign was brief.

It must be remembered that all these little events and scores of similar ones were purely incidental. Our real business, our most absorbing interest, was, of course, helping to get the academic program of the University under way. Meetings and conferences, consultations with students, questions of policy to be determined at once—all of these by themselves would have filled the days. The University was insisting on entrance examinations; and the students were working themselves up into the conventional frenzy and had to be given sympathy, as well as not too conscious restraint. At last, however, the memorable day came, October 1, 1892, when the exercises were held which formally opened the University and made our pulses throb as we realized what those readings from the Scriptures and hymns and prayers might signify to the educational world.

We were then ready to settle down to our work as students, for that we all were. In spite of the many difficulties in the new situation, the principles which Mrs. Palmer and I had recognized as fundamental in the rational organization of the social and domestic life of University women became a part of the conscious life of the group. Too great credit cannot be given to those students who co-operated in evolving from their experiences very real contributions to the richness of the common life. My young secretary, Antoinette Cary, who had been a student at Wellesley College, and who became, in June, 1893, the first student to take the degree of Bachelor of Science from the University of Chicago, served as a kind of liaison officer and smoothed over many rough places. Under the influence of young women of fine ideals, generous social attitudes, and high scholarship, there arose gradually, and in accord with the principles which had been recognized, a set of unformulated customs.

All through the winter of 1892–93 the little community at the Hotel Beatrice realized that they were transients and would have to vacate by April 15 in order that the building might be made ready for World's Fair tenants. It was a merry and a motley company that made a continuous procession to Snell Hall during those moving days. Lamps and vases, dustpans and brooms, party dresses and overshoes, toilet articles and perfumery, all the articles which were difficult to pack, were carried without hesitation in the open.

And, again, it was an unfinished building. Again no lighting fixtures; no entrance steps, but a plank to walk; no front door; only one tap from which water could be drawn, and sixty women needing toilet facilities. But everybody was in good spirits, as I had occasion to learn from the complaints which came to me about the noisy gatherings which made sleep impossible until morning hours, and about which something had to be done. The situation was difficult, for one of the most prominent leaders was an intimate personal friend and college mate of mine, who, after some years of teaching, had come to the University as a graduate student and was enjoying the sense of freedom from routine and responsibility. Then was sown the seed whose fruitage soon became a distinguishing and greatly admired characteristic of the University of Chicago. I called together all the residents and explained what our objectives should be in such a domestic community, and asked that the occupants of each floor should meet and choose three of their number to serve as their representatives in conducting the affairs of the group. Pending their action, I appointed a temporary committee and placed my friend upon it. The result was as I expected. Although without much experience in dealing with groups of people, I had already begun to realize that comparatively few people fail to measure up to responsibilities which are placed upon them. This belief was amply confirmed as the years passed, and led to the conviction that most of the objectionable conduct of young people is due to the fact that they are not given duties and responsibilities worthy of their intelligence and energy.

Those spring months at Snell Hall were an exciting experience for us all. The rapid developments of the University first of all kept us on the *qui vive.* Kent Chemical Laboratory, within a few rods of Snell Hall, was rapidly taking form. We were greatly distressed early one morning when a teamster, working over hours because of financial distress, was thrown from his lumber-laden wagon, which was upset in the rain-soaked, soft ground. He was brought into Snell Hall and found to be seriously injured. We cared for him until medical services could be secured and he could be removed by ambulance.

All the time there was the excitement of preparations for the opening of the Columbian Exposition. The University Council, the highest administrative body of the University, had its dignity upset at a certain session when a member, looking out of the window, exclaimed, "The Ferris Wheel is moving!" All business was stopped so that the long-anticipated sight could be admired.

The neighborhood rapidly took on the characteristics of a locality dominated by a great public attraction. Prices rose steadily day by day. Students found it difficult to find suitable eating places. Even the accommodations furnished in the dark and damp basements of the divinity halls and the Hungarian goulash and corned beef and cabbage served there were not very alluring, so little groups of students were organized to furnish their food in their own rooms. One group took turns in doing the marketing. It was reported that lamb chops, which everybody wanted, cost altogether too much. One day the market woman said she had found some at a reasonable price, and the group proceeded to cook and enjoy them and voted to have more very soon. But alas! the next buyer returned with a sad tale. The relished chops had been pork, not lamb! Previously each one had declared that never, under any circumstances, could she eat pork!

My room was on the first floor near the entrance. One night I was much disturbed by a man and woman who lingered, talking and laughing in such a manner that all the sleepers on that side of the hall could but be kept awake. At 2:00 a.m. I thought the limit had been reached, and so, clad in my wrapper, I went to the door and requested the woman to come in. She was very indignant—quite furious, in fact. It interested me some years later, on meeting her casually, to have her tell me that she had realized how thoughtless she had been that night and that I had been more than justified in putting a stop to her conduct. I thought it was fine of her, and after that I always had a high opinion of her.

Finally the Spring Quarter closed and our experiences in roughing it were theoretically ended. The permanent Women's Halls were to be occupied when the University reopened October, 1893.

The procedure which had been followed at Snell Hall formed the basis of the House plan which was adopted by the Trustees in June, 1893. The general rules were as follows:

1. Composition of a House:
   a) Members of the University entitled to continuous residence in a particular Hall shall constitute a House.
   b) Residence in a Hall is limited to students in attendance on courses in the University, and officers of the University.
2. Officers:
   Each House shall have a Head, appointed by the President of the University; a Councilor, chosen from a Faculty of the University by the members of the House; a House Committee, elected by members of the House, of which House Committee the Head of

the House shall be chairman and the Councilor a member *ex-officio*; and a Secretary and Treasurer elected by members of the House. Each House, through its Committee, shall make a quarterly report to the President. A House may select, with the approval of the Board of Student Organizations, one or more persons not directly connected with the University as patrons or patronesses.

3. Membership: The residents in a Hall shall be members or guests.

   a) Membership shall be determined by election under the respective House By-laws. Election of members shall take place not earlier than the end of the sixth week, nor later than the tenth week.

   b) In cases of vacancies, the Registrar shall have power to assign applicants to rooms in the order of application. Students thus assigned shall be considered guests, and if these guests are not elected to membership during the first quarter of residence, they shall have no further claim upon the rooms occupied. The room rents will be fixed and collected by the University. The privilege of membership in a House may be withdrawn by the Board of Student Organizations, on recommendation of the Head and Councilor.

4. Rules: Each House shall be governed by a body of rules adopted by a two-thirds vote of the members of the House and approved by the Board of Student Organizations.

The "rules" provided for were merely a mode of procedure and were called "House Customs." The following were those approved by the Council, June 23, 1893:

1. As much quiet should be maintained in the corridors and rooms as is practicable, especially in the evenings.

2. The House shall be closed at 10:15 p.m.; all who wish to enter later than that hour should make arrangements in advance with the Head of the House.

3. Academic students wishing to be away from the House in the

evening shall consult with the Head of the House in advance, and provide for suitable chaperonage.

4. As far as possible, Friday and Saturday evenings only shall be considered as reception evenings. It is preferred that callers, especially callers from the Quadrangles, should not be received on Sunday.

5. Guests cannot be entertained over night in the students' rooms, but other rooms will be furnished if practicable. Gentlemen may be taken to students' rooms only by permission of the Head of the House.

The freedom implied in these "Customs" was in marked contrast to the elaborate code of "rules" which prevailed in other institutions, and its practicability was seriously questioned by other deans. After explaining its meaning at a conference, I heard a dean say, on leaving the room, "She may be able to do it with her girls; I couldn't with mine." She did not realize how alike girls are the world around.

In accordance with the House plan, the students who had been in residence in 1892–93 and who returned after the Summer Quarter, during which the University buildings had been given over largely to Columbian Exposition visitors, were organized into three Houses and took possession of the three new "residence halls" (the approved substitute term for "dormitories")— Kelly Hall, Nancy Foster Hall, and Beecher Hall. Green Hall was not opened until November, 1898. Miss Myra Reynolds and I were the Heads, respectively, of Nancy Foster Hall and Green Hall; and Miss Elizabeth Wallace and Miss Fanny C. Brown were joint Heads of Beecher House. One of the characteristics of the system was that the social direction of the Houses should be by women of academic position.

It is interesting to note that the rental of rooms was from $25.00 a quarter up to an average of about $40.00, and the initial charge for table board was $3.50 a week. And there were com-

Afternoon tea in Beecher Hall: Evelyn Matz, Edith Foster, Harriet Agerter

plaints about the high charges, as there have been continuously ever since and doubtless always will be.

Even after two experiences, pioneering days were not yet over. Unfurnished, and even unfinished, buildings were again to be academic homes. Nancy Foster Hall was so far from completed that its residents were obliged to go to Kelly Hall for several weeks and seek the hospitality of its dining-room. The open fireplaces in certain sleeping-rooms seemed to present undue advantages; but when it was found that the flues would not draw and masonry had to be torn down in the walls of the newly furnished rooms in order to remove the obstacles in the flues, the envious residents retired to their quiet and clean quarters with a feeling that there were compensations for them.

The Halls presented certain common features of physical and domestic accommodation as well as similar forms of business administration. Each had its separate dining-room, its own rooms for social intercourse, and each provided, in the main, single bedrooms.

Mrs. Ellen H. Richards, of the Massachusetts Institute of Technology, a close friend and adviser of mine, suggested that the University should try some improved methods of feeding students. She transferred to the University the equipment of the Rumford Kitchen which she had established at the Columbian Exposition as a means of showing scientific and economical methods of preparing food. She gave what was still more valuable. Her generous contribution of experience and time made a success of the experiment of a central kitchen, although it was conducted under very unfavorable conditions. Aided by Miss Sarah E. Wentworth, she showed that the system promised results in efficiency and economy; and the experience paved the way to the establishment of the University Commons.

In spite of optimistic anticipations, complaints about the food were not infrequent. Differences in eating habits, overwork, eating between meals, late hours, and other factors made the problem of giving satisfaction to everybody almost insoluble. Time and experience brought gains; but it seems probable that there will always be individuals, usually not of cosmopolitan experience, who will complain that their peculiar tastes are not gratified. It proved not difficult to substitute fruit and cereals for meat and potatoes at breakfast, but the process of making soups and salads (oil! bah!) acceptable was a slower one. I remember distinctly an interview I had with a woman fellow who was making much trouble with her complaints. I learned gradually that she was enrolled for more than the approved number of courses, was working on her Doctor's thesis, never took any exercise beyond the limits of the Quadrangles, slept poorly, was under extreme financial pressure, and—worst of all—was carrying on her work in defiance of her family's expressed wishes. I then took up the matter of trying to give her satisfaction in regard to food and told her that she would have to change practically all the other conditions before it would be probable that we or anybody else could provide food which she would enjoy.

The new groups proceeded at once to organize under the House plan. It was understood that each House should have its own traditions and customs and cultivate an individual spirit, bearing in mind the principles on which they were founded, viz., unity, liberty, and social responsibility. The different Houses immediately took on individual characteristics. Special note may be taken of Miss Reynolds' leadership during a long period of years. She gathered about her personal friends of distinction and charm. Strangers of eminence visiting the University were frequently entertained. There was created a social atmosphere which was much enjoyed and appreciated by the students. The effect upon them was noticeable. In spite of the fact that many of them had had but limited social experience, many observers might be found to corroborate the opinion of a certain guest that she had never met, in any part of the world, young women who had more agreeable social manners and at the same time such marked mental alertness and serious purpose. In a similar way Miss Wallace in Beecher Hall and I in Kelly Hall were devising ways and means of enriching the House life and at the same time showing how personal freedom could be harmonized with the best social standards.

The years passed, bringing their problems and their interests grave and gay; and experience strengthened the conviction that in the administration of the Halls the break away from the more or less rigid rules and supervision which were in force in other institutions had been fully justified. Mrs. Kelly's gift in memory of her parents enabled the University to fill the gap between Kelly Hall and Beecher Hall, where the foundations for a building had already been laid; and on November 13, 1898, Green Hall was occupied by a small group of students, with me as Head. No other Hall was opened until the summer of 1909, when Greenwood House across the Midway was organized, with Miss Langley as

Head. On October 11, 1917, Drexel House was formed, and an added element of self-help was introduced. At the beginning of the summer of 1918, Woodlawn House was organized as an experiment in maintaining a residence without facilities for a common table, and in the following year Kenwood Hall was added to the list. The lapse of time has but served to emphasize the demand for more Halls, and confirm the desirability of providing further means for caring for the domestic needs of the women students of the University in such a way as to make their intellectual resources more effective.

The primary objective of the Residence Halls was naturally to secure physical conditions favorable for the work of students, and incidentally to give them opportunity for social experience and the enrichment of personal relationships. That we were successful in giving University work the first place was proved at least in more than one case, where sisters chose to attend different universities, one basing her decision on the greater academic opportunities offered, while the other preferred the attraction of sororities, social functions, and other forms of social amusement.

Our aims involved: freedom directed by intelligent choice; consideration for others; a determination on the part of each to choose a path not only worthy of the University but conforming to one's own best ideals, rather than to drift heedlessly or to conform to unfitting, but possibly popular, standards. I often had occasion to point out that many students had a desire to do active social service work and that it was doubtful if they would ever find themselves in a community of from forty to seventy persons where there were so many and constant opportunities for friendly and considerate service. Naturally, a fine spirit of co-operation was necessary and it was in most cases forthcoming; and it was recognized that activities which might interfere with the rights of others, such as the use of musical instruments and typewriters, loud talking and laughing, and visiting back and forth, should not be countenanced. It was often pointed out that failures to co-operate were not really due to the euphemistic term "thought-lessness" but, in the final analysis, to straight "selfishness."

By various methods the House spirit was maintained and even strengthened; and there were few cases when freedom in the intellectual, as well as in the social, life was abused. But the confusion in social standards which came with the World War, and which still exists, affected the University of Chicago as it did all groups of young people, though much less seriously than it did most college communities. Increasingly late hours, an excessive amount of social life, and various types of failure to appreciate the obligations of membership in the University led President Judson to question whether the time had not come to place more restrictions upon the students in the Women's Halls. (Parenthetically, it may be noted that again Eve was to be held solely responsible!) I informed the women in the Halls of the action suggested and expressed my profound regret that the system which had brought much satisfaction and commendation was seriously threatened. The women accepted the challenge and worked out a plan by which more positive measures could be taken to inform the fast-succeeding groups of newcomers of the standards of the University. The plan agreed to by representatives of the different Houses at a very solemn conference was acceptable to the President and was put into operation at once. Its essential provisions were the appointment of a social committee in each House to take upon itself the responsibility for interpreting to the new women in each Hall the spirit and traditions of the House and for discussing with all residents social standards and conduct. The result of the system, or perhaps more truly of the agitation caused by the suggested restrictions, was entirely satisfactory, even though there were occasionally found in the student groups individuals who lacked good breeding and were unwilling to show social consideration for others. The situation is one which calls for constant watchfulness. It is true, indeed, that "eternal vigilance is the price of liberty." In this case the vigilance manifests itself through the general high morale of the group and their appreciation that true freedom comes through self-control.

This account of the salient features of House organization among the women of the University of Chicago and the special features of life in one Hall shows but in part the possibilities of the system. President Harper expressed his opinion of it in the following words: "The time will come when every student of the University will be a member of a University House. The development of the University life is largely dependent on the growth of University Houses."

That this opinion is generally held by the authorities of the University is proved by the fact that every plan for the increase of living accommodations for women students is based on the House system. It is true that those who have lived in the Halls for any considerable period of time can recall difficult and perplexing episodes, instances of not altogether creditable conduct, and evidences of ill-breeding and selfishness. On the other hand, those who hold the skeins of such memories in their hands have more than enough by far to offset them in the messages and impressions which come from time to time. "It was a turning-point in my life," say the young. "For the first time since I left home to teach was I happy and reaching my ideals of intellectual and social companionship," say the old.

The Weaker Sex

During the decade preceding the opening of the University, a band of college women had been studying ways and means of giving to women freer entrance into the field of scholarship. The Association of Collegiate Alumnae, organized in January, 1882, and known after 1921 as the American Association of University Women, took as its first objective the improvement in the health of college women, since it was popularly believed that women were not physically able to bear the strain of a college education. This undertaking had been no more than started when, at its second meeting, the Association proceeded to investigate the subject of graduate study for women in spite of the view frequently held that women were not mentally equal even to college work.

Women had some grounds for confidence in their intellectual ability. Helen Magill (later Mrs. Andrew D. White) had taken the degree of Doctor of Philosophy at Boston University in 1877 and was the first woman in the United States to hold that degree. In 1884, Cornell University awarded a fellowship to a woman, Harriet E. Grotecloss, and gained distinction as the first institution in the United States to make such an award. These were, however, exceptional instances, whereas fellowships were readily available for young men whereby they might go to Germany or some other country for the advanced work in research which was not as yet generally attainable in the United States. Assistance and encouragement were given to young men who might choose to be fitted to hold teaching positions in the colleges and universities throughout the land. But very few graduate courses of any kind were open to women, and no positions on college faculties outside of the women's colleges could be obtained by them. It was a distinctly masculine procession that was advancing into the field of research and scholarship. There was plenty of work for the Association to do, and they set about it valiantly. They little dreamed that within two or three decades the Association would be holding endowments for more than ten fellowships and a little later would be well on the way toward securing a fund of one million dollars for the further endowment of national and international fellowships.

But for a long time the road was a hard and weary one to travel; and there was but slight hope that, even if women were well equipped in scholarship, places would be found for them among the groups of scholars in the universities. Every appointment, even to a laboratory assistantship, was a source of cheer and gave encouragement to the belief that such a footing would lead the way to higher positions. But in whatever direction one turned, the way seemed blocked. The world seemed to have forgotten that several centuries before women had held, with distinction, professorships in leading universities of the Old World.

Such was, in brief, the status of women scholars in academic life when the educational world was startled and the Association of Collegiate Alumnae greatly heartened by the announcement of the new University of Chicago that women were appointed on its faculty and as fellows. Three months before the University opened, the first number of the *Quarterly Calendar*, dated June, 1892, gave the names of the following women as members of the prospective staff: "Alice Freeman Palmer, Ph. D., Litt.D., Professor of History and Acting Dean [of women] in the Graduate School of the University Colleges; Julia E. Bulkley, Associate Professor of Pedagogy and Dean [of women] in the Academic Colleges; Zella Allen Dixson, Assistant Librarian; Luanna Robertson and Elizabeth C. Cooley, Academy Tutors; Alice Bertha Foster, M.D.,

Elizabeth Wallace

Tutor in Physical Culture; S. Frances Pellett, A.M., University Extension Reader in Latin." There were also six women fellows announced: "Senior fellows: Mabel Banta and Myra Reynolds; Junior fellows: Elizabeth Wallace and Mary Frances Winston; Honorary fellows: Maud Wilkinson and Madeleine Wallin."

In the following September two new names appeared on the Faculty list, viz., Martha Foote Crowe, Ph.D., Assistant Professor of English Literature; and Marion Talbot, A.M., Assistant Professor of Sanitary Science and Dean (of women) in the University Colleges. The distinction between senior and junior fellows disappeared in this same issue of the *Calendar,* and the names of Julia B. Platt and E. Antoinette Ely were added to the list of honorary fellows.

This was the situation when the University opened October 1, 1892. No wonder the road ahead seemed clear. But the vision proved to be somewhat of a mirage. No new appointments of women and no promotions were made for two years. In 1894 the wheels seemed to move, for Elizabeth Wallace, who had been a docent for a year, was promoted to a readership! In 1895 Myra Reynolds, who had held an assistantship for one year, became an instructor, and I was advanced to an associate professorship. There was, however, no woman even nominally a professor, for Mrs. Palmer, at the end of three years of advisory service, retired from her connection with the University. In 1896 Kate Anderson, who had succeeded Alice B. Foster, was raised from a tutorship to an instructorship. In 1897–98 there were eleven women of all grades on the Faculty—a merely nominal increase in proportion to the enlarged number of men. The years that followed proved to be rather dark ones for women, although no whispers were heard against their efficiency and devotion. A few bright spots should be noted. I was made a professor in 1904. Sophonisba P. Breckinridge, who was fellow in political science from 1897–1901, was docent in the same department from 1902 to 1904, and instructor and assistant professor in household administration from 1904 to 1920, when her distinguished career in social service administration began officially. Ella Flagg Young was an outstanding member of the Faculty from 1899–1904. Gertrude Dudley's inestimable and memorable services began in 1898. Edith Foster, who began as assistant in English on her graduation in 1897, reached, as Mrs. Flint, a professorship in 1923 and occupied many positions of trust and responsibility. Elizabeth Wallace's story was almost parallel, and her influence and activity of great value. Edith Abbott, who had an appointment in the University as fellow in 1903, came again to the University in 1914 as lecturer in sociology and in 1920 was appointed associate professor of social economy. Later, as Dean of the Graduate School of Social Service Administration, she began the magnificent work which has placed the

Edith Foster (Flint)

School in the front ranks of social-welfare schools. In 1901 the organization of the School of Education brought a considerable addition of women to the teaching staff, notably Zonia Baber and Alice Peloubet Norton. When the medical work was developed, several women appeared on the scene, but mostly as assistants.

The list of women who have contributed to the upbuilding of the University must close here, although among those not named are some not less distinguished.

Meanwhile the professorial groups were increasing very rapidly in the number of men, several of those who had reached the highest professorial grade having received their baccalaureate degrees later than women, who were still held in the lower ranks. Had the women failed to make good; and, if so, were there not others who might replace them?

Some comments on the situation may have interest.

Among the twenty women who held fellowships in 1899 and the two following years are eight whose names appeared in *Who's Who in America* in 1935, besides three who were listed in *American Women*, the official women's *Who's Who*. Fifty-five per cent to achieve national recognition is a gratifying proportion.

Generalizations concerning women in the field of scholarship have offered frequent opportunity for investigation. One instance resulted from the statement of a University professor known to be sympathetic with the aims of young women scholars. He said, in a public address, that both the wish and the ability of young women to take a college course had been abundantly proved (and consequently the old charge of their unfitness had been disproved); but, he went on to say, except in rare instances they showed little inclination to pursue their studies in the Graduate School. What did a study of the recorded facts show as to the validity of personal impressions? By that time the University had conferred the Bachelor's degree on 700 men and 598 women. During the preceding year, July 1, 1902–July 1, 1903, 88 of these men and 85 of the women had enrolled as members of the Graduate Schools of Arts and Sciences, or 12.6 per cent of the men and 14.2 per cent of the women were pursuing their studies. It was significant that of the 88 men, 10 were holders of fellowships, while of 85 women only 3 had been granted this assistance in continuing their studies.

Another statement was made to the effect that, in general, women who pursue higher studies are not so persistent as men and their scholarship is not of so high a grade. The statistics of the University showed that the first point was true, but the difference was surprisingly small. Of the 377 men who had held fellowships, 153, or 41 per cent, had attained the degree of Doctor of Philosophy. Of the 76 women who had held fellowships, 27, or 36 per cent, had received the same degree. In view of the limited opportunities and few inducements open to women scholars, it was rather surprising that there was not a greater difference.

In regard to the scholarship of those who had received the doctorate as determined by the grade of the degree, the accompanying table, compiled at the same time (1903), proved interesting. It shows that, while a slightly larger percentage of women than men fall in the two lowest classes, the percentage of men in the very lowest class is much larger than that of women. The figures for the highest class are slightly in favor of the women. It must be remembered, however, that with so small a total number of women a difference of even one in either the highest or lowest class would make a very appreciable difference in the percentages of those classes. In spite of these, and other creditable records, little advance was made in giving recognition to women.

	MEN		WOMEN	
	Number	Per Cent	Number	Per Cent
Rite	58	22.4	5	10.4
Cum laude	91	35.1	24	50.0
Magna cum laude	94	36.3	16	33.3
Summa cum laude	16	6.2	3	6.3
Total	259		48	

In December, 1924, the latent discontent among the women came to a crisis, and the three women who held professorships out of a total of 150 decided that drastic action must be taken, and, after careful deliberation, addressed the following communication to the President of the University and the President of the Board of Trustees:

GENTLEMEN:

The undersigned women members of the University Senate beg leave to call certain matters to your attention and ask your consideration of them in connection with plans for the future development and administration of the University. Their deep interest in the University and their loyalty may be measured in part by the ninety-five years of their joint connection with it.

I. The articles of incorporation include among the objects for which the University exists, the following:

To provide, impart, and furnish opportunities for all departments of higher education to persons of both sexes on equal terms.

These objects seem to us to be not adequately fulfilled in the following respects:

a) There is no woman on the Board of Trustees.

b) The Faculties of Arts, Literature, and Science have on their teaching staff too small a proportion of women, not even furnishing a sufficient number to fill the positions of Deans and Heads of Houses.

c) Although women comprise over 40 per cent of the graduate students and show by the grades accompanying the doctorates they receive that they reach a very high plane of achievement, they receive only about 20 per cent of the fellowships, including special fellowships designated for women.

d) Of the University of Chicago Bachelors who received the Doctor's degree between 1919 and 1923, seventeen received appointments to the Faculty. Seven men received appointments of professorial rank and the two women in this group received instructorships.

e) Promotions and increase of salary are awarded to women more slowly than to men. There are three women Faculty members who received their Doctor's degree in 1907 or earlier and who are still only associate professors; whereas twenty-one men who received their Doctor's degrees in 1907 or later hold full professorships. No one of these men has received the honorary degree of Doctor of Laws, whereas two of the women have received it.

II. The slight rôle given to women in "providing and imparting opportunities for education to persons of both sexes on equal terms" is supplemented with slight recognition given to them in other academic relations, viz.:

1. There have been 134 convocations with but four women orators.

2. Only one honorary degree has been conferred upon a woman.

3. Only twice has any woman been asked to speak at homecoming or Trustees' dinners.

4. With very rare exceptions women are not invited to give University Public Lectures.

5. Women do not receive appointments on important Faculty committees.

6. Women are not always represented in social functions given in the name of the University.

7. Women of the Faculty are given no opportunity to enjoy or to offer hospitality except under strict limitations at the Quadrangle Club.

8. No opportunity has been given the Faculty women to aid in working out plans for the development of the University, especially as it concerns the women of the University.

III. In view of the preceding facts we would urge—

1. The appointment of a woman Trustee.

2. The appointment to the Faculties of several women of distinction and power in scholarship, teaching ability, or administrative skill.

3. The granting of greater encouragement to young women scholars of promise.

4. A larger recognition of women in semi-academic ways.

5. Better facilities for agreeable social life.

6. Further opportunity to make known the needs of women

Faculty members and students which either exist today or will be felt in the near future.

We believe that the measures here proposed will work advantageously in raising the status of young women students in college activities and that they will tend to produce even more women graduates of distinction and a body of women whose influence on boys and men through the school and the home will bring to the enrichment of the University a stream of young and able youth.

Finally, the University of Chicago, if true to the ideals on which it was established, can make a great contribution through the encouragement it gives its women members, toward the development of those resources of the world which are in the keeping of women and which they are called upon more and more to contribute to the progress of civilization.

[*Signed by*]   *Edith Foster Flint*
Marion Talbot
Elizabeth Wallace

We waited with some trepidation for the repercussions from this bolt. A formal acknowledgment came from President Burton, but no more definite response. A rumor reached us, however, that the communication was read to the whole Board of Trustees and its statements were challenged. One member claimed that if any of the alleged facts were untrue or were misrepresentations, all the signers should be at once dismissed. A special committee was appointed to learn whether the statements could be verified. Their report was that the statement was not only true in every respect but might have been made even stronger. The women were gratified when, on the next announcement of promotions, Miss Abbott, Miss Katherine Blunt, and Miss Breckinridge were named as professors. Some other results followed, such as the appointment of a woman as Convocation orator; but on the whole no great progress was made.

Sophonisba Preston Breckenridge

The need of more women skilled in administrative matters and interested in promoting this phase of the University's activities has not yet been met, greatly to the detriment, as many observers believe, of the women students. It may be added that a fairer recognition of scholarly women would not only have a good influence on the younger students—but would widen the competition, thus raise the marginal level, and even do the men scholars some good, though it is possible that neither men nor women would be conscious of any altruistic motive underlying such a policy.

This brief résumé of the participation of women in the work of the University gives little hint of the whole-hearted devotion they showed. With hardly an exception, they worked as a team for upholding and advancing the intellectual and social standards of the University. Their common goal had no trace of self-seeking. Their common objective was the constant subject of their discussions and conferences. According to the notion current in some quarters, it might be assumed that differences of opinion would lead to petty personal antagonisms, or even spite. Many occasions, however, occurred when visitors from other academic groups were impressed by the friendly atmosphere and the devotion to a common cause which gave creditable and rare distinction to the group.

This résumé of the history of women on the Faculty has its disheartening aspect and seems to confirm the widespread conviction that present-day conditions offer little opportunity for women to receive recognition for their intellectual and administrative gifts. Discouragement is quite general, but here and there the battle cry is heard. The women of today must not falter in claiming the right to use their powers, and they will find more to encourage than to dishearten if they scrutinize this sketch of what has happened at Chicago in less than forty years. At the beginning the outlook was black indeed. The difficulty, if not impossibility, of believing that there were to be women on the Faculty of the new University may be shown by a little incident. Shortly after the University opened, the ladies of a neighboring church invited the Faculty and their wives to a Turkey Dinner. The invitation addressed to Mr. and Mrs. Marion Talbot was delivered to me. Nobody disputed my right to the share of the dinner, which I enjoyed. A glance forward of only twelve years from that time shows a woman holding a seat in the highest educational body, the Senate, of an institution which had a right already to a place among the great universities of the world. God's mills do not always grind slow, and history may be a tonic when courage and hope waver.

CHAPTER EIGHT

Forward Steps

When I returned from a series of interesting visits in eastern cities during the winter following my graduation from Boston University in 1880, I continued my studies for the Master's degree, which I received in 1882; but I missed the regular routine of college life and, even with my parents' help, could not see very clearly what interests should claim my time and strength. Fortunately, in the fall of 1881, a vision came to my mother of a union of the few women who at that time had graduated from college. I consulted Mrs. Ellen H. Richards, who had graduated from Vassar College in 1870 and was teaching at the Massachusetts Institute of Technology. We summoned for conference the few college women whom we knew, including Alice E. Freeman, the young president of Wellesley College; and in January, 1882, the Association of Collegiate Alumnae was formed and I was chosen to be its secretary and served in that office for thirteen years, or until my election to the presidency.

Since many people, especially physicians, were objecting to collegiate training for women on the ground that it was physically disastrous, the Association took up, as its first topic for investigation, the health of college women. Soon after, a group of members, including Ellen H. Richards, Alice Peloubet (later Mrs. Norton), and myself, formed a sanitary science club. Mrs. Richards was naturally the leader and stimulated Mrs. Norton and myself to go on with our studies in the welfare of the home

---

and the household. I continued my studies at the Massachusetts Institute of Technology and, in 1888, received its degree of S.B. In 1889, I was asked to give a series of lectures on sanitation to the students at Lasell Seminary. It is interesting to note that I called their attention to a new theory of disease which had recently been suggested and which was called the "germ theory." I told the students that it had not been generally accepted, but it would be worth while for them to note whether it made any progress. In 1890, through the initiative of my close friend, Alice Freeman, now Mrs. Palmer, I was appointed instructor in domestic science at Wellesley College and for two years gave to the Seniors a three-hour course including house sanitation and dietetics. In the meantime, as secretary of the Association of Collegiate Alumnae, as a member of the Board of Visitors of Wellesley College, as secretary and later president of the Massachusetts Society for the University Education of Women, and as alumni trustee of Boston University, I had been studying rather closely various problems involved in the collegiate education of women.

As plans took shape for administering the new University of Chicago, Mrs. Palmer told me about what was involved and said that she wished me to assist in organizing the life of the women students and be a full member of the Faculty. When the offer came from President Harper, it was to be assistant professor of sanitary science and dean (of women) in the University Colleges. I was to teach the subjects in which I had prepared myself and had had experience; but, as there was to be no domestic science department in the University, my courses were to be included in the Department of Social Science (later Sociology). Then came one of the most gratifying experiences of my life, a letter of welcome from Professor A. W. Small, head of the department, written in his characteristically cordial manner and without a trace of condescension or irritation because this strange young woman, with her, at that time, non-academic subject, had been administered into his Department. I was given full recognition, even to being named as one of the board of editors of the *Journal of Sociology*, when it was established.

In the meantime, my friend, Alice Peloubet, had married Professor L. M. Norton; and, on her husband's death, leaving her with five young children, she had begun teaching. She met with such great success that when, with the financial support and intelligent co-operation of Mrs. Emmons Blaine, Colonel Francis W. Parker left the Cook County Normal School in 1900 to organize the Chicago Institute, he selected Mrs. Norton to be a member of the faculty. She spent a year in further preparation for this special work.

Meanwhile there had been much discussion throughout the East as to the proper term to apply to the range of subjects connected with the activities of the home. A group of actively interested persons, meeting at Lake Placid in September, 1899, agreed to discard the various terms which had been in use, and to adopt the term "home economics." When the University established the School of Education, of which the Chicago Institute was a constituent part, Mrs. Norton continued her teaching under the general term of home economics and offered courses in 1901–2.

Early in 1902, I submitted to President Harper a plan for a department of household technology, choosing the term on the analogy of departments in other fields. I proposed an increased staff of instructors, laboratory facilities, enlarged equipment, a practice house, a fellowship and scholarships, and possibly a journal. President Harper stated that he thought "the plan a strong one"; but, as so often in those days when the University's enterprises were outrunning the limits of its purse, a compromise had to be made on the ground that no extra funds were available. We then issued a bulletin on *Courses in Household Technology and Related Subjects.* The opening statement read:

The University of Chicago offers special courses dealing with the problems of the home and the household. The instruction is intended to give men and women, as a means of liberal culture, a general view of the place of the household in society, to train men and women for the rational and scientific administration of the home as a social unit, and to prepare teachers. Fundamental courses in physics, chemistry, physiology, bacteriology, political economy, and the study of society are given.

Then followed a list of courses offered by Assistant Professor Norton, Associate Professor E. O. Jordan, Assistant Professor Albert P. Mathews, Associate Professor George E. Vincent, Professor Charles R. Henderson, and myself. This plan was followed for two years.

In 1904 the time seemed really ripe for the establishment of a new department. President Harper this time gave his approval. My courses were withdrawn from the Department of Sociology. Miss Sophonisba Preston Breckinridge, who had just completed the course in the Law School (the first woman to take its degree of J.D.) after having received the doctorate in political science, had shown great interest in the legal and economic aspects of the household. She and I thought that these subjects had been almost completely overshadowed, if not ignored, by the emphasis placed on food and clothing, although in the changing conditions of industry and society they were becoming increasingly important. In order to show the changed emphasis which the new department wished to place on studies relating to the home, it was given the new name of Department of Household Administration. Mrs. Norton was made assistant professor of the teaching of home economics in the School of Education and assistant professor of household administration in the Faculty of Arts, Literature, and Science. She had charge not only of the courses in teaching but of the courses in foods which involved laboratory experimentation. Dr. Breckinridge was appointed to an instructorship and offered courses on legal and economic interests of the home, while I retained the sanitary and social aspects. The first bulletin announced courses chosen from those given in the School of Education and the Departments of Sociology, Chemistry, Zoölogy, Physiology, and Bacteriology, as well as a series of special lectures on varied aspects of family life given by some of the most distinguished members of the Faculties.

The most significant part of the bulletin was, however, the introductory statement. It read in part as follows:

> Students of social movements look with apprehension on present-day tendencies which draw men more and more in the direction of commercialism and women into industrialism to the detriment of home and family life and the consequent injury of the larger social interests of which it is the foundation. . . . The University of Chicago announces the establishment of a Department of Household Administration. . . . Theoretical courses dealing with the economic, legal, sociological, sanitary, dietetic, and aesthetic interests of the household will be supplemented by practical work, all to be conducted on a strictly collegiate basis.

In this undertaking a new note was certainly struck. It was characteristic of the University of Chicago not to be bound by the academic traditions of the past. No other college or university had ventured far from the beaten path in home economics. Cooking and sewing still represented to them the essential interests of the home.

It is a satisfaction to record that the University of Chicago was the first institution to offer courses which recognized that the great changes in industry and in political and social organization called for corresponding changes in training for family life. The home was rapidly becoming a consuming, rather than a producing, center. This called for less study of methods of domestic manufacturing and more study of those industrial and governmental institutions through whose agency the householder is enabled to care more effectively for her family and household.

Dr. Breckinridge offered courses in the "Organization of the Retail Market"; "Standards of Living"; "Consumption of Wealth"; "Relations between the Householder and the Public," as represented by federal, state, and municipal authority; "Standards of Child Care"; "Legal and Economic Position of Women"; "Care of Families in Distress"; while I offered "The House as a Factor in Health"; together with courses on the social, economic, hygienic, and legal aspects of dietetics and the administration of the modern household.

But it may be true, as one observer remarked some years later, that the note was struck a quarter of a century before people were ready to heed it. To change the metaphor, the seed, however, was planted; and though it was slow in coming to fruition, at the end of a quarter of a century it suddenly bloomed and everywhere were evidences that family relations and the well-being of the household were recognized as subjects demanding careful study and worthy of an honored place in a university curriculum. In the intervening years the University was either too handicapped financially or too fearful of increasing the proportion of women students to take any steps toward the enlargement or strengthening of the Department. It had a reasonable number of enrolments, more than in some and fewer than in other departments; and among the students were several who later became distinguished for their leadership. No special change in the organization of the Department took place until 1913, when Mrs. Norton withdrew from the School of Education, greatly to the regret of her many friends. After a short period, when Miss Agnes K. Hanna directed the work in the School of Education, Dr. Katharine Blunt took the position and retained it until her acceptance of the presidency of Connecticut College for Women in 1929. On my retirement in 1925 and the appointment of Dr. Breckinridge to a full-time professorship in the School of Social Service Administration, the Department of Household Administration in the Schools and Colleges of Arts, Literature, and Science and the Department of

Home Economics in the School of Education were combined, except that the courses in the teaching and supervision of home economics were retained in the School of Education—an arrangement which was prevented years previously only because of the peculiar circumstances which attended the introduction of the work. The titles of the two departments were united in spite of the manifest cumbersomeness which resulted.

Anyone interested in studying the development of domestic activities and the relation of the home and the family to the community can but note the changes which have taken place in the type of training which schools and colleges have offered. It is not too much to claim that the University of Chicago has had a vision of needed changes and given an impetus to a movement which is already bearing rich fruit.

CHAPTER NINE

The Dean of Women

The English language is not unlike other tongues in containing many words which have several different meanings. One may speak, for example, of a "captain," meaning of a regiment, a football team, a steamer, a squad of bell boys, or even of industry. The duties and responsibilities—and uniforms—are different in each case. The same is true of the term "dean." For example, my father was dean of a school of medicine; my brother, dean of a cathedral; and I, dean of women in a university. I think, however, that my niece, aged six years, stretched the term to its limit. On her way to Chicago to visit the Columbian Exposition her mother heard her tell some ladies in the sleeping car that she was going to visit her auntie who was dean of the World's Fair. "No, Margaret," her mother called across the aisle, "that isn't what Aunt Marion is." "Oh, no," the child said, "auntie isn't dean of the World's Fair—she is dean of the Universe."

The functions of the dean of women vary all the way from those of a full teaching member of the Faculty holding the highest rank, both administratively and academically (the position which I was so fortunate as to hold) to those of an upper housekeeper or merely a chaperon. Before the University of Chicago adopted the term "dean of women," the office had different designations, where it existed at all. "Lady principal," "principal of the women's department," "adviser of women," "preceptress," and "lady assistant" were among the terms used.

The selection and organization of the Faculty of the University of Chicago forms an interesting chapter in its history. An important phase was the selection of women to assist in the administration. The action which was taken soon resulted in the establishment for the first time of the office of dean of women. On February 23, 1892, Julia E. Bulkley was elected by the Trustees, associate professor and Academic (later Junior) College dean. In 1895 she took up her residence at the University. In the interim her name had appeared in the published lists of the Faculty as associate professor of pedagogy and dean (of women) in the Academic Colleges. She remained in the same position until 1899, when she became dean in the College for Teachers. The following year she resigned.

In his search for an experienced administrator who would give especial aid in organizing the life of the women students, President Harper realized that the outstanding woman in the country was Mrs. Alice Freeman Palmer, formerly president of Wellesley College. President Harper's efforts to secure her aid and to persuade her husband, Professor G. H. Palmer, of Harvard College, to become head professor of philosophy, were not successful; but Mrs. Palmer agreed to give her assistance for a part of each year. On July 25, 1892, she received her appointment and thereafter for three years her name was published as professor of history and dean (of women) in the Graduate School and College, with a footnote as follows: "Mrs. Palmer will reside at the University, in all, twelve weeks during the year; she will, however, while absent, retain an active share in the administration." Mrs. Palmer held this position for three years.

In the meantime, President Harper felt the need of having a woman permanently charged with the duty of directing the academic, domestic, and social life of the women students; and on August 31, 1892, the suggestion of Mrs. Palmer that I, who had been her colleague in the early years of the Association of Collegiate Alumnae, be appointed to serve was adopted by the Trustees, and I was made assistant professor of sanitary science and dean (of women) in the University (i.e., Senior) Colleges. Except during the comparatively short periods when Mrs. Palmer was in residence, I took the entire responsibility, including the registration of all women students. In 1895, I was promoted to an associate professorship and became dean (of women) in the Graduate Schools. In 1899 I was appointed Dean of Women. The announcements for 1897 and 1898 stated, "There are also two deans of women, one for the Graduate Schools and one for the Colleges." This was followed in 1899 with the statement, "There is also a Dean of Women." This was the first time the term was used in any institution. I was promoted to a professorship in 1905 and held this position and the deanship until my retirement in 1925.

Mrs. Palmer and I agreed that we would not favor having the women separated from the men in the awarding of degrees and consequently would not urge that the dean of women should present the women for the degrees. As the position of dean of women was one of responsibility, we laid stress on the importance of a dignified recognition of the fact by having her sit with the highest administrative officers on public occasions.

Before I left home for Chicago, my mother said to me, "Marion, do not forget that, as dean, you will be an administrative officer; it will be your duty to carry out regulations made by authorized bodies, not to make regulations yourself." Many, many times have I had occasion to thank her for this counsel; and many, many times have I been grateful that, because of it, I have escaped difficulties which have befallen other deans of women. When I have heard them say, "I made such and such a rule," "My rule is so and so," in describing their procedure, I have gasped with dismay but have not wondered that they have met difficulties.

Another bad situation arises when the president of a college announces a rule ex cathedra for the dean of women to enforce without having had any previous conference with her. It was my good fortune to have been on such terms with the presidents of the University that, so far as I knew, they never proposed any action affecting the women students or the social activities of the University without conferring with me in advance. President Harper went even further. Once when a question of jurisdiction came up, he said, "That is for Dean Talbot to decide—all matters concerning women belong to her"; and such views he expressed to me in writing. This made my task no small one; but, at the same time, it made me very careful to heed my mother's warning. Over and over again students would come asking for exceptions to University rules. I would say, "I have no authority to make an exception; you should petition the proper board or committee either through its secretary or through me"; and occasionally I would have to say, "Frankly, I shall not favor granting your request, but the board may not agree with me." It is a source of constant gratification to me that my counsel was always listened to with courtesy by my associates. If we did not agree, sometimes one side would yield and sometimes another; but it seemed to be the general view that in my field my views should prevail. This again made me careful to discuss questions of administration very frankly and fully with my colleagues in advance of action.

There were, however, occasions when I had to use my general blanket authority as understood by President Harper. One day I noticed from my office that his daughter, very grotesquely garbed and carrying a market basket, was walking outside and attracting attention and ridicule. I sent for her and learned that she was being initiated into a club. I said she must go home and attire herself properly for public gaze. Then I talked with the president of the club, pointed out that more strangers, especially from foreign countries, passed in and out of the University doors than those of any building in Chicago, except possibly the Auditorium Hotel (then the leading hotel of the city), that they were all critical of the University and especially of the women, and we could not afford to tolerate conduct which might amuse a small and intimate group but which reflected no credit on this group in the eyes of the public. Her justification was that men did such things and she understood that women had the same rights as men in the University. My reply in turn was that women had the same rights as men to do anything creditable, but no rights at all to do anything discreditable, even if the majority of the men set the example. Word was evidently passed about, for thereafter such features of initiations, if they were approved at all, took place in private. Such experiences made me very reluctant, in fact wholly unwilling, to have a new rule passed whenever an objectionable situation occurred. A much better way seemed to be to advise with the student concerned. This was, of course, a long-drawn-out process; but I doubt if it consumed more time or effort than would have been necessary to enforce a body of minute rules and, moreover, it resulted in the development of a kind of morale which was very effective. "It isn't done" proved more of a deterrent than "It's against the rules." It was in this way that the term "co-ed" never came to be used by our community; and that "women of the University" was substituted for "girls of the University," commonly used in other institutions. I made a strong point of this because I was much impressed when Professor Salmon of Vassar College pointed out how disadvantageous it was to women to use the terms "college men" and "college girls."

There was one serious objection to the system which I have often heard phrased by students in this way: "I like it here, but I miss the fun of breaking the rules," or "Girls don't win prestige here by breaking a rule and getting away with it." A rather significant incident showed how the force of public opinion worked. An Irish Catholic student, who had been brought up in a convent under very strict discipline, entered the University a little late. She was vivacious and attractive and soon tried to establish especially friendly relations with a group of fellow-students whom she evidently admired. One day she said to them, "What do you do when you want to meet a man you have been forbidden by your parents to see?" The expression on their faces must have shown that that way of climbing the social ladder was a failure. The story reached me. I was quite baffled. I had no experience with that type of problem. I chose the easiest way and did nothing but keep informed as to those of her doings which were easily observed. A young man called the next Sunday afternoon, and she went out with him. She returned about eight o'clock. The young man never called again. He may have done something which showed that he was really not a fit companion. She may have met already more attractive men. Most probably, the charm of successfully evading a rule was broken. It was fortunate that the whole episode covered only two days, for detective work and espionage were not my forte or to my liking.

Occasionally the question of organized student government came up. I never favored it. There were several reasons. First, I had observed that in some instances, if not in all, the students did not really govern except in very trivial matters which did not interest them. Second, if theoretically they had great power, practically the Faculty pulled the strings. This situation led once to a serious revolt in another institution—in fact, almost disrupted the college. Third, the time consumed in making and enforcing rules made serious inroads on the students' working time and strength. Fourth, it is a serious question whether it is a proper or desirable function for students officially to discipline and punish each other. Fifth, and to my mind the chief reason, government, in the sense of a penal code, has no place in a group of intelligent people working with common intellectual aims on a rational social basis, any more than it has in a family of ordinary intelligence and with common interests.

As I have said, the duties and opportunities of the office of dean of women vary greatly in different institutions. When it was established at Chicago, there were no precedents to serve as guides. A carte blanche order had to be filled. Fortunately, my own resources were generously and sympathetically supplemented by suggestions and aid given by other officers of the University, of whom I would name with special appreciation Deans

MacClintock, Capps, Vincent, Angell, Lovett, and Robertson, Mr. W. A. Payne and Mr. F. J. Gurney. Nevertheless, each situation as it arose had to be met in general on an individual basis. It may be imagined that if all the situations and problems had appeared simultaneously they would have been overwhelming. Fortunately, it was not long before I realized that it would be futile to pass much general legislation to regulate procedure, since there seems no limit to human ingenuity in evolving social problems. A solution is no sooner found than its further need seldom appears, but one for a different question becomes pressing. Nevertheless, when it came time for my retirement and I was asked to prepare a statement concerning my activities, I was able to present a brief outline as follows:

PARTIAL SURVEY OF INTERESTS AND
DUTIES OF THE DEAN OF WOMEN

General policies concerning women by—
1. Correspondence, i.e., giving information concerning conditions of living, methods of administration, forms of organization, candidates for special scholarships, social life, etc. answering questionnaires, following up newspaper stories
2. Consultation, i.e., advice as to relations with women's undertakings such as Naples Table, deans of women, Association of University Women, etc.
3. Attendance at meetings of Faculties and Boards and recommendations for action

Graduate women:
Promotion of Women's Graduate Club
Hospitality to women fellows
Consultations as to plans, etc., of graduate women

Organized social life:
Recommendations to Board of Student Organizations
Registration and approval of social functions
Direction of social calendar
Conferences with social committees and officers of organizations
Assistance to fraternities in maintaining good social standards
Lists of members of women's secret clubs
Approval of proposed new members
Conferences as to methods of administration of clubs
Assistance in forming organized groups
Consultations with officers of organizations (e.g., Y.W.C.A.)

Publicity and hospitality:
Arrangements for women guests and speakers. Entertain-
    ment of women visitors
Representation of women of the University at meetings, banquets,
    on advisory boards, etc.

Women's Halls:
Assistance in choosing Heads of Houses
General co-operation with Heads of Houses
Help in meeting perplexing situations in Halls
Chairman of Inter-House Council

General social and personal matters:
Standards of dress, dancing, conduct, and manners
Consideration of unfavorable criticisms
Requests from non-University people and organizations for co-
    operation
Conduct of men in Women's Quadrangle
Women's activities in sales contest and other money-raising under-
    takings
Advice about money matters
Conferences as to occupation, marriage, etc.

Complaints of landlords, employers, etc., lack of conveniences in
   buildings, insults, offensive conduct, thieving
Aid in accident, illness, death, mania, etc.

The foregoing outline indicates the large part that social direction played in the duties of the office. It was always subordinated
to the intellectual interests of the University and the well-being
of its members as students. The following principles were formu-
lated quite early in the history of the office of dean of women and
were used to the fullest possible extent in taking official action
and giving personal counsel:

The social life is to be so ordered as to (1) contribute to, and
not impair, the intellectual efficiency of the students; (2) be a
source of physical recreation and not of bodily exhaustion; (3)
add to social resources of students and to their ease and enjoyment in meeting different social situations; (4) develop a sense of
social responsibility and dependableness; (5) aid in establishing
reasonable standards of money expenditure; and (6) include as
many students as possible who need it.

While intellectual achievement was my ambition for the men
and women of the University if they were to prove worthy of
the devotion, ability, and sacrifices which were poured into the
making of the University, it was also perfectly clear to me that
fine social standards and activities were contributory factors in
this achievement. Without them the utilization of intellectual
equipment provided at such cost would be greatly lessened, if not
wholly prevented. Such is the teaching of sound psychology, and
to its end I was content to give my constant and best attention.

CHAPTER TEN

The King of France

The King of France went up the hill
With twenty thousand men;
The King of France came down the hill,
And ne'er went up again.

One fine day in 1902 when the world seemed to be going on its way quite serenely, a member of the Faculty, walking on Lexington, later University, Avenue, noticed that on the lot north of the President's House some timbers had been placed upright at regular intervals about a large area. Shortly afterward, meeting Professor Shorey, he said, "Have you seen the President's hen coop that is going up?" "Hen coop," flashed back Professor Shorey, "coup d'état!" Evidently something dramatic was happening. Would it turn out to be a tragedy or a farce? Perhaps after more than a generation one can judge from the following description of the plot and action which it was, if either.

Title: Co-education versus Segregation

Scene: The United States
Actors: President Harper
Prominent professors with daughters not interested in intellectual pursuits
Small but resolute group of Faculty determined to have real, not pseudo, co-education

A still smaller group nurtured at eastern men's colleges deadly opposed to co-education

Large majority not especially interested but good-naturedly acquiescing in the plans of the administration

A large body of fighting alumnae

Chorus of newspapers, educational journals, and college and university authorities scattered throughout the United States

Plot: Substitution of separate instruction for co-instruction of the sexes in the University of Chicago.

The length of the play covering a period of three years of constant action naturally precludes verbatim repetition in this place. A bare outline will have to suffice.

Scene 1: Original agreement of organizers of the University (1892), viz., that "the privileges of the institution be extended to persons of both sexes on equal terms."

Scene 2: Separate sections for men and women suggested by President Harper in his annual report for 1899.

Scene 3: At the meeting on July 3, 1900, of the University Congregation (that grandiose organization which never lived up to President Harper's expectations and, after a period of coma, finally expired) the following topic was recommended for discussion:

Resolved, That better educational results would be secured in the University by teaching the sexes in separate classes. This question was amended by the Executive Committee March 20, 1901, by changing the term "University" to "Junior Colleges" and was discussed by the Congregation on the same day when it was referred to the University Council for consideration and report. The Council, however, did not take up the discussion of the question.

Scene 4: Discussion by the President and members of the Board of Trustees and sketches of the proposed Women's Quadrangle were prepared by the University architects.

Scene 5: The President requested the Senate on October 12, 1901, to postpone a vote on a motion to divide the attendance of Junior College students at Chapel Assembly alphabetically, instead of by sexes, as was being done.

Scene 6: Discussions by the Senate at five different meetings.

Scene 7: February 1, 1902, the Senate voted 13 to 8 in favor of having the Trustees accept a gift of a million or a million and a half dollars for the erection of buildings for women, with recitation halls and laboratories exclusively for women in the Junior Colleges, the plan having been considered by the Trustees on January 28 and later on February 18, 1902, adopted unanimously by the Trustees, including the plan to organize the work of the Junior College women as a separate division.

Scene 8: Great outpouring of protests and petitions from widely scattered alumnae and friends, with voluminous correspondence and editorials in newspapers and journals.

Scene 9: Agreement by President and Trustees to reopen whole question for discussion and separate it from any financial consideration.

Scene 10 *et seq.:* Series of meetings of Junior College Faculty, Senate, Congregation and Trustees, votes of disapproval, reconsideration, changing of votes, votes of approval. The Congregation finally decided to acquiesce in the plan.

On October 22, 1902, the Trustees took final action as follows:

The action of the Junior College Faculty recommending that, in the development of the Junior College instruction, provision be made as far as possible for separate sections for men and women, having been presented to this Board by the President of the University, with the indorsement of the University Senate, and the various protests and objections on the part of the friends of the University interested in the subject to the recommendation, together with a memorial of protest from members of the Faculty, having been duly read and considered:

It is resolved that the recommendation of the Junior College Faculty and Senate of the University, reported to the Board by the President of the University, be approved and adopted as the action of this Board; and the President of the University is requested to formulate a plan for its practical administration and present the same to the Board for its approval.

Fifteen of the Trustees were recorded as favoring the action and four as opposing it.

What was the cause of the turmoil? The alleged reason was the overcrowding of Cobb Hall, which made the development of plans for the Colleges seem timely, if not pressing.

The rapidly increasing proportion of women undergraduates was creating alarm in certain quarters and, in the opinion of one at least who heard the discussions of small responsible groups, was more truly the cause of the proposition than were some of the other alleged reasons. The proportion of women students to men students was 24 per cent in 1892–93. For the following years the proportion was: 33 per cent; 35 per cent; 36 per cent; 37 per cent; 38 per cent; 1898–99, 43 per cent; and in 1901–2, 52 per cent.

It is worth noting that in 1898–99, 50 men and 52 women received honorable mention, honor scholarships, and honors in departments. An explanation of this situation is hinted at in the remark of a bumptious young man student who was serving as a messenger in one of the administration offices, "No man can lower himself by competing with girls in the classroom."

One way of meeting this danger, as I pointed out at the time, was to make the University more attractive to men. Within three or four years the following means of serving men were inaugurated: Bartlett Gymnasium, Reynolds Club, Hutchinson Commons, Hitchcock Hall, the Law School, and the School of Commerce and Administration.

President Harper, calling himself (after experience in institutions for men only, women only, and for both men and women) a strong believer in co-education, expressed himself as confident that important progress was to be made in this department of educational thought and practice. He believed that "the forward steps should include at least (1) a closer definition of the term itself; (2) a larger elective privilege on the part of the women as to the extent to which they shall or shall not mingle with men; (3) a similar larger election on the part of the men; (4) a larger possibility for the cultivation of what has properly been termed the 'feeling of corporate existence' in the institution concerned on the part of both men and women; (5) a larger opportunity for cultivating the life which is peculiarly woman's life and, on the other hand, the life which is peculiarly man's life."

President Harper was also quoted as saying: "Certain limitations have already clearly fixed themselves. It is not deemed proper that men and women should take physical exercise together in the gymnasium." (Note that they could swim together in the ocean and dance together on the ballroom floor even though, in the latter case, the costumes of women were much scantier than was allowed in those days in the gymnasium.) "It has never been proposed that they should occupy the same halls or dormitories." (Note: Hotels have not been administered on the segregation principle.) "The controlling aim in constructing the Women's Quadrangle should be to secure privacy and convenience in the matter of going from halls to classroom (bathrobes and pajamas *de rigueur*). The controlling aim in constructing the Men's Quadrangle should be to provide for intermingling and close association.

"The first buildings to be erected in the Women's Quadrangle should be: a certain number of halls for residence, the gymnasium, a clubhouse for women, one hall for non-residence Houses, and one building which could be used for classrooms and laboratories. The first buildings to be erected in the Men's Quadrangle should be: a building to be used for classrooms and laboratories, a hall for non-residence Houses, halls for residence." (Note: Observe order in which provision was to be made for intellectual training.)

Finally, at the word "Go!" the system started with the Winter Quarter, 1903. The machinery creaked, for only 2 per cent of the men in the Junior Colleges were segregated in all their work and 35 per cent of the women. One wonders if this shows a greater desire on the part of the women to keep aloof from the men! On the other hand, 43 per cent of the men and 25 per cent of the women had no separated courses. The rest had one or two separated courses. A generalization made by Dean Vincent that "the separation of instruction affects nearly four-fifths of those registered in the Junior Colleges" shows that the meaning of these statistics might be read one way or another according to the bias of their interpreter. The Dean, however, went on to say that in the Spring Quarter the numbers whose work was wholly in separate sections were almost negligible. The Dean drew some other significant conclusions from two years' experience: First, "it meets most of the objections against throwing suddenly into constant association large numbers of young men and women just leaving home and entering on a new experience." (Note that practically all these young people were from co-educational high schools. The private-school graduates, for the most part, were the ones who had any startling emotions at taking part in a class recitation or listening to a lecture in the presence of members of the opposite sex.) Further, "it does not seem to have affected unfavorably the general social life of the institution"—in other words, intellectual association (acquaintance ships were seldom formed in class) was more disturbing than social companionship such as dancing.

In spite of every reasonable effort to maintain segregated sections, the practical difficulties in administering the system were seen in its gradual abandonment by one department after another until for several quarters Freshmen English had to bear the onus of the system; but in time this course, too, gave way, and the whole thing quietly died. Nobody attended the obsequies, and nobody took note of them. Even the excited and indignant alumnae, who had protested by all kinds of measures, from letters of indignation published in the daily press to dignified appeals to various officers of the University, paid no attention to the quiet ebbing of interest in the scheme. They did not even say, *"De mortuis nil nisi bonum."*

When a decade had passed, I felt it safe to make a visit to a neighboring state university which I had very unintentionally, even unconsciously, offended. During the period when Boards, Faculties, Senate, and Congregation were in almost continuous session, I did not dare absent myself from a single one in which I had a seat. I had accepted a very friendly invitation to spend a week-end at this university. On the day before I was to start, a notice came of a special meeting of the Junior College Faculty. I could not risk being absent, for the sword of Damocles was over the heads of the women. I telegraphed to the university that I was detained by urgent business. The next issue of their student paper contained one of the most vituperative articles I ever saw, and I was the object of it! After all, the only business for which this special meeting was called proved to be to act upon some technical details in regard to the adjustment of a few students' records to the requirements for graduation.

And what of the King's palace, the hen coop, Lexington Hall? It became greatly endeared to the younger women of the University even when, as it aged, its occupants had to use skill in avoiding water dripping from leaking roof and floors dotted with puddles. Women's organizations found quarters there; chapel services were held there for a time until the fear of some of the Faculty was allayed that the walk to Mandel Hall would overtax the women; dances, banquets, many activities, went on in both the Hall proper and the adjoining gymnasium, with its grassy court. At first any men who were privileged to enter the building did so with becoming modesty. Even the instructors modified their air of male superiority. But the strain was too great. As the instructional scheme broke down, so did the plans for the building. One day we discovered that men students were using a room where they met Faculty wives in conference about costumes for a Blackfriars performance. The ladies sewed and fitted, and even laced young men into corsets. With perhaps a little black malice in our hearts we raised the question as to this use of the building, even though the room was situated near an entrance door not much used by women students. We were asked not to press the matter—it would not recur. This was, however, the beginning of the end. Typewriting offices, bakery, mess hall for Student Army Training Corps, the *Maroon*, gradually took possession of the main building; while the gymnasium, after a period of use by the Nursery School, became the headquarters for the Reserved Officers' Training Corps. Lexington Hall had outlived its usefulness for women, and few remember now its original function, though many women look upon it, even in its decrepit condition, with affection.

So the King of France went up the hill and—down again.

A Dream Come True

The composite mind of the thirty-five hundred women who by 1914 had received degrees from the University of Chicago would have a memory of the location of their physical-education headquarters and gymnasium in the following terms: October, 1892, a room on the fourth floor of Cobb Hall; November, 1892–June, 1901, the north end of the temporary library building on the present site of Hutchinson Court; June, 1901–October, 1901, a frame building on Ellis Avenue; October, 1901–October, 1902, the Sunday-school room of the Hyde Park Baptist Church; Autumn Quarter, 1902, the south end of the old library building; Winter Quarter, 1903, the gymnasium of the School of Education; April, 1903–1916, Lexington gymnasium.

The many discomforts and difficulties which were met by the students did not dampen their interest but rather added ardor to their desire to help secure an adequate building for a gymnasium and other purposes. Through penny races, circuses, and varied ventures they made brave efforts to raise the needed money. During this disheartening period, the Woman's Union, the Young Women's Christian League, the Women's Athletic Association, the Neighborhood Clubs, as well as smaller groups, developed a spirit of friendliness and of enterprise, as well as frequently of merriment, which was destined to be recognized in a munificent manner.

The story of how the donor was interested and the gift secured was a genuine romance, and the few persons who were privileged

Mrs. La Verne W. Noyes

to hear it from the lips of the President's wife were fortunate indeed. Mrs. Judson had frequently told of her desire to have an adequate woman's building which would give the facilities to the women which Hutchinson Hall, Bartlett Gymnasium, and the Reynolds Club had given to men since 1903. Very late one evening in May, 1913, Mrs. Judson, feeling restless and unable to sleep, had a sudden thought. She recalled the recent death of Mrs. La Verne W. Noyes, a personal friend; and like a flash it occurred to her that Mr. Noyes might be interested in presenting a Woman's Building to the University as a memorial to his wife. She seated herself quickly at her desk, wrote a note to Mr. Noyes laying the suggestion before him, threw on a wrapper, cast the fateful document into the letter box on a nearby corner, and hastened back into the house. It was the witching hour, darkness and quiet were her only witnesses, and, above all, the President was out of the city. Alarm seized her, for it was an act of temerity; but contrition was futile, the deed had been done. In fear and trembling and yet in hopeful expectancy, she awaited the reply. It came by the return mail, asking for an interview, the result of which placated any reproach the President might have felt inclined to feel when on his return he learned what had happened.

A few whispered confidences, an air of great mystery, and speeches with enigmatical phrases at the annual dinner of the Woman's Athletic Association in June, 1913, were the precursors of the President's stirring announcement before the vast crowd assembled for Convocation in Hutchinson Court on June 10, 1913, that Mr. La Verne W. Noyes had made a gift, as a memorial to his wife, to take the shape of a building devoted to the social and physical life of the women of the University. The enthusiasm of the women was intense, and the sympathetic applause of the men was a gratifying gauge of the unified spirit of the University. "The good of each is the good of all" was the note one could hear resound through the tumult of cheers and clapping. Mr. Noyes's letter of presentation read as follows:

1450 Lake Shore Drive
Chicago, May 31, 1913

Dr. Harry Pratt Judson
President, University of Chicago
58th Street and Ellis Avenue, Chicago

DEAR SIR:

Pursuant to our conversation, I write to say that I will pay to the University of Chicago, in instalments as hereinafter mentioned, a total sum of Three Hundred Thousand Dollars ($300,000.00) for the construction, on a site to be agreed upon, on the campus of the University of Chicago, in this city, of a building to be used as a social center and gymnasium for the women of the University. It is understood that this building is to be a memorial to my deceased wife, Ida E. S. Noyes, and is to be known as the "Ida Noyes Hall."

The character and plans of the building and the construction of it I shall leave to the discretion of the Trustees of the University, but I shall be glad to co-operate with them in any way that seems desirable.

Yours very truly,

[*Signed*] *La Verne Noyes*

The following action had been taken by the Board of Trustees on June 4, 1913:

Resolved, That the letter of Mr. La Verne Noyes dated May 31, 1913, and addressed to the President of the University, be spread on the Minutes.

Resolved, That his gift of $300,000 for a women's building to be erected in the Quadrangles of the University be accepted under the conditions and for the purposes contained in the letter aforesaid.

Resolved, That the thanks of the Board of Trustees of the University of Chicago are extended to Mr. Noyes for this splendid benefaction to the cause of education and especially to the welfare of the women students of the University.

Resolved, Further, that the Board, while deeply appreciating the magnitude of the gift, feels especially gratified that there is to be commemorated in the Quadrangles of the University the name of a gracious and gifted woman whose rare qualities are well worthy of admiration and emulation of successive generations of our young women.

Finally, it is the confident expectation of the Board that the Ida Noyes Hall will be an important addition to the University Quadrangles, not only as in itself a stately structure, but as affording opportunities for great service in many ways to countless students in the long ages to come.

The President of the University is instructed to convey this action of the Board to Mr. Noyes.

The first problem to be solved in making the new building a reality was the choice of a site. This was not a simple matter, as it involved many difficult problems connected with the future development of the University. A final decision was not reached until after the President's return from a summer in Europe. Finally, from several lots submitted to Mr. Noyes for a choice, all of which he personally inspected, he selected the south side of the block bounded by Fifty-eighth and Fifty-ninth streets and Kimbark and Woodlawn avenues. This choice made the building one of the prominent group facing the Midway, and insured a type of building adequate to its purpose as well as a fitting memorial.

Meanwhile suggestions as to the building itself were sought from all quarters. An outline of the needs to be met was made, and plans were sketched on the principle that the building was to be essentially a unit with each of its parts so related as to make the whole available for the greatest number of needs of the greatest number of people. On October 27, 1913, Shepley, Rutan, and Coolidge were appointed as architects, and they proceeded at once to make tentative sketches based on the preliminary work.

Gertrude Dudley

A commission of University women was appointed by the President to make a study of the plans as they developed. The following constituted the commission: Mrs. Harry Pratt Judson; Marion Talbot, Dean of Women; Gertrude Dudley, Director of the Women's Gymnasium; Myra Reynolds, Mary J. Lanier, Elizabeth Euphrosyne Langley, Heads of Women's Halls; Sophonisba P. Breckinridge, Assistant Dean of Women; Elizabeth Wallace, Dean of Junior College Women; Geraldine Gunsaulus Brown, Caryl Cody, Julia Dodge, Young Women's Christian League; Pauline Sperry, Ethel Preston, Woman's Graduate Club; Nancy Miller, Florence Foley, Helen Furchgott, Miriam Whalin, Marjorie Coonley, Ruth Victorson, Neighborhood Clubs; Isabel MacMurray, Louise Mick, Woman's Athletic Association; Cornelia Beall, Arline Brown, Ruth Hough, Charlotte Viall, Suzanne Fisher, Letitia Fyffe, Margaret Riggs, Helene Pollak, Margaret Rhodes, Harriet Tuthill, University aides; Ruth Hough, Dorothy Llewellyn, Dorothy Farwell, Undergraduate Council; Lucile Bates, Women's Glee Club; Mrs. Nott Flint, Mrs. Ethel R. MacDowell, Marie Ortmayer, Josephine Turner Allin, Alumnae.

Tentative sketches were placed on exhibition in Lexington Hall. The president of the Reynolds Club, the president of the Dramatic Club, and other men of the University made interesting and helpful suggestions. The inevitable result followed. With the perfecting of the details, and especially with the adoption of an architectural standard befitting the site selected for the building, the original gift proved inadequate and was most generously increased. The total gift of Mr. Noyes amounted to approximately half a million dollars.

The architects submitted plans and specifications embodying the suggestions of the commission and others, January 29, 1914. The plans were accepted by the Board of Trustees, February 4, 1914. The contract was let to Wells Brothers Company, December 18, 1914. On November 19, 1914, ground was broken. Nine days later the first work was done in laying the foundations. According to the contract, the foundations were completed and ready for cut stone work on January 15, 1915. The cornerstone was laid on April 17, by Mr. Noyes in the presence of a large company of Trustees, Faculty, students, and friends of Mr. and Mrs. Noyes. After an introductory statement by President Judson, I made a brief address, closing as follows:

> I speak not only for myself but for all the women of the University when I assure you, Mr. Noyes, and you, Mr. President, that this cornerstone means a mighty impulse toward the truly great things of life. Here self-discovery and self-control will lead to social co-

operation and mutual understanding. The weak will learn from the strong, and the strong will learn from the weak. Tolerance, sympathy, kindness, the generous word, and the helpful act, all typical of the woman we commemorate, will be the contribution of the women who go forth from Ida Noyes Hall to take part in the up-building of the new civilization which is to come.

Meanwhile, with almost the first sign of big building operations, a new problem confronted the Trustees. Architects, engineers, and contractors with designs, estimates, and computations, and gangs of men with picks and shovels were not the sole craftsmen interested. Not only in Chicago, but all over the land, every type of house-furnishing and interior-decorating establishment was quick to see the opening for interesting and profitable business. Nearly overwhelmed with insistent attempts to secure the contract for furnishing and equipping the building, and puzzled by the wide variety of aesthetic and practical standards proposed, the Trustees sent the following letter on June 21, 1915, addressed respectively to Miss Marion Talbot, Miss Elizabeth Wallace, Miss Myra Reynolds, Miss Gertrude Dudley, Miss E. E. Langley, and Mrs. E. F. Flint:

DEAR MADAM:
You have been appointed by President Judson a committee from the Faculty to confer with the Committee on Buildings and Grounds of the Board of Trustees with reference to the selection of furniture for Ida Noyes Hall. The chairman of the latter Committee is Mr. C. L. Hutchinson.
                    Very truly yours,
                        [*Signed*] *J. S. Dickerson, Secretary*

I was appointed by the Trustees chairman of the Advisory Committee. Formal work was not done until after the Summer Quarter. On October 11, 1915, the Committee met in the President's office and, in conference with him, decided upon certain general principles to be followed. The consideration of details, almost infinite in variety and perplexity, occupied every spare minute of the working days. Long evening sessions were necessary, and even some sleeping time was given to the interesting task. The result was the production of a seventeen-page typewritten document containing a list of articles, with estimated price, needed for each room in the building, the total for the three different divisions of the building—clubhouse, gymnasium and physical-education department, and refectory and kitchens—amounting to $71,500.54. The Committee had used charts drawn to scale for each of the rooms and, with movable blocks representing different articles of furniture, even to rugs, had worked out in great detail the choice and placing of every article. This had been followed by an estimate of the costs involved. The report of the Committee was submitted to the President on November 24, 1915, accompanied with the following letter:

NOVEMBER 24, 1915

President H. P. Judson,

DEAR SIR:

The Advisory Committee on the selection of furniture for Ida Noyes Hall begs to submit the accompanying recommendations. The Committee has held frequent and prolonged sessions. The members have conferred with experts in furnishing as well as with individuals and groups of persons interested in having the Hall furnished in an appropriate and beautiful way and also with a view to securing the greatest degree of comfort and efficiency for the activities which are to go on in the Hall.

It is needless to say that the members of the Committee will be glad to serve further in any way in their power.

Very sincerely,

[*Signed*] *Marion Talbot, For the Committee*

The following reply was received:

Office of the President
CHICAGO, NOVEMBER 29, 1915

DEAR MISS TALBOT:
Thanks for your report on the recommendations of furniture for Ida Noyes Hall. I will lay the matter before the Committee immediately. May I take this occasion to express my appreciation of the very strenuous work which the Committee has done, and which will certainly go a long way toward making the Hall livable?

Very truly yours,

[*Signed*] H. P. Judson

DEAN MARION TALBOT

THE UNIVERSITY OF CHICAGO

On November 30 the Committee on Buildings and Grounds of the Board of Trustees voted "to recommend to the Board of Trustees that authority be given to the Advisory Committee of Women to select and purchase furniture and equipment for Ida Noyes Hall at a cost not to exceed $72,000, that in connection with this purchase there shall be consultation and co-operation with the University Purchasing Agent, and that in connection with the furniture and furnishings of the Refectory there shall be consultation and co-operation with the Director of the University Commons."

Here was a challenge to a group of women whose time was already filled with professional duties. But visions of the ill-adapted, unattractive, and costly schemes for furnishing the building which had been proposed served to offset any qualms they might feel. The challenge was accepted, and the group entered at once upon their labor of love. Mrs. H. P. Judson, Mrs. Martin A. Ryerson, and Miss Cora Colburn were soon made members of the Committee. It was necessary to act with dispatch, as war conditions were bringing rapid advances in prices and no rate could be guaranteed for more than a few days. In some cases advances were made overnight. Specific duties, including the selection of goods, were assigned to each member of the Committee; but all selections were made subject to approval by Miss Langley, whose technical knowledge, experience, and fine taste led to the confidence of the Committee and were large factors in the ultimate success of the work.

It was natural that, as time proceeded, some changes were seen to be desirable in the projected plan. Architectural difficulties were met, market conditions offered obstacles, certain decisions were postponed until nearer the completion of the building; but on the whole the scheme proved to be very satisfactory as the work advanced. The very careful and painstaking buying led to such savings that some improvements were found practicable, as, for example, the substitution of oriental rugs for Austrian hand-tufted rugs.

The following procedure was agreed upon:

After selection is made, a requisition for the approximate amount is drawn, signed by the chairman of the Committee, and certified by the Purchasing Agent. It is understood that Miss Talbot will withhold signature to the request for purchase until approval is given by the member of the Committee most directly concerned. The requisition shall then be presented to the Committee on Expenditures of the Board of Trustees. On receiving their approval Miss Talbot's final authorization will be given to the Purchasing Agent, who will issue the purchase order and attend to the routine of checking delivery of goods and passing bills.

Very frequent meetings of the entire Committee were held for consultation and the decision of uncertain questions. Each member was provided with a copy of the proposed scheme. The accompanying table illustrates the general scheme which served as a guide.

As each purchase was completed, an entry was made on the master copy which I kept. Accordingly, at any time there was definite knowledge, not only of how the work of selection was progressing, but of how the financial account stood. Occasionally, favorable purchases resulted in a saving which could be transferred to another item whose cost proved unexpectedly large; but this was never done without the consent of the Committee. As the result of the painstaking efforts of those employed in the task, involving even such arduous expenditures of time and strength as trips to the Atlantic and Pacific coasts for the purpose of making favorable purchases, the outcome of the labors of the Committee was not only an equipment which harmonized with the building in usefulness and beauty but an expenditure about three thousand dollars less than the appropriation—an almost unparalleled achievement in the history of such enterprises.

PROPOSED SCHEME FOR PARLOR G ALUMNAE ROOM

1 rug, 9 × 9 feet	$108.00
1 rug, 12 × 12 feet	192.00
1 divan, 6 feet	150.00
1 divan, 5 feet	65.00
1 divan table	45.00
1 nest of tables	30.00
1 table with leaves	25.00
1 desk	35.00
1 desk chair	15.00
4 easy chairs	120.00
10 chairs	100.00
1 jardiniere	10.00
1 jardiniere stand	15.00
1 candelabrum	12.00
2 vases	5.00

1 tea cart	25.00
1 scrap basket.	3.00
2 pairs of curtains	70.00
4 cushions	25.00

Ida Noyes Hall was dedicated and opened on June 5, 1916. On June 17, 1916, the chairman of the Committee received the following letter:

JUNE 17, 1916

Miss Marion Talbot
Faculty Exchange
MY DEAR MISS TALBOT:
At a meeting of the Board of Trustees, held June 13, 1916, it was voted, in view of the fact that most of the furniture for Ida Noyes Hall had been selected and that members of the Committee will be absent or engaged in full-time teaching, that hereafter it will not be necessary to ask the Advisory Committee of Women to undertake the purchase of additional furniture. From this date, therefore, the Advisory Committee of Women will serve as an Advisory Committee and not as a committee to purchase.

I am sure that the Trustees desire to have me express hearty thanks to all the women who have devoted so much energy and efficiency to this important task. The beauty of the building has been much enhanced by the character of its furnishings.

Yours very truly,

[*Signed*] *J. S. Dickerson, Secretary*

Please notify the other members of the Committee.

In November, 1916, President Judson sent to the chairman a communication in which, after expressing the sincere appreciation of the University of the valuable work done by the Advi-

Ida Noyes Hall

Scene from the Masque

sory Committee and outlining the various steps which had been taken in the organization of the work, he said: "The faithful labors and excellent judgment of the various sub-committees have had their result in the beautiful and commodious provision made for the Hall in its present operation." After formally discharging the Committee, the letter closed with the phrase, "The Committee is entitled, may I again say, to the cordial thanks of the University."

In this story about Ida Noyes Hall no attempt has been made to cover the whole subject. The official reports which have been published tell of the beautiful Masque and other brilliant features of the dedication on June 5, 1916. Nor can it do more than hint at the gracious hospitality and fine standards of the social director, Mrs. G. S. Goodspeed, or the gatherings, both grave and gay, which took place in it, or the appreciation expressed by visitors from all parts of the world, who were unanimous in considering it the finest building for women in the country.

The Great War

The women of the Faculty met immediately on the declaration of war by Congress to decide upon the measures for giving service to be recommended to the women students. On April 16, 1917, the women students gathered in Mandel Hall to hear the proposals by which they might share in the defense and preservation of the nation. It was a momentous occasion, one of the most important meetings ever held in the University, as well as the most thrilling and solemn. No factitious appeal was made, no time was given to sentimentalism or weak emotion, no flags were shown, no cheers measured the depth of response; but everyone present felt the thrill of patriotism and the genuine significance of the occasion. As the years passed and the conviction grew of the worse than futility of war—not only of the World War, but of every war—there could but be regret for the waste of such noble emotions as were shown on this particular occasion. We did, however, the best we could; and as I look back, I think we did not make as many mistakes in judgment or so-called "patriotism" as was the case in some other communities.

It was my responsibility to conduct the meeting. I said that the Faculty women realized that the students wished to give loyal service but were at a loss to know how best to do it. They knew they were not fitted to be war nurses. Many were not interested in making surgical dressings or comfort kits. They had all seen how wasteful and useless much of the knitting had been. I told them how, under the leadership of Mrs. Judson, the President's wife, the women of the Faculty, the wives of members of the Faculty, and neighbors had been organized as the University of Chicago Women's War Relief. It seemed essential for the students to avoid the mistakes which had been made by women in other countries. One of these was duplication and consequent waste of effort. It seemed best to leave them free to make use of any agencies already organized, but we had prepared a special program based on the following principles:

1. The United States is at war and the losses and burdens inevitably entailed will fall most heavily upon women, upon whom also will rest in consequence a large responsibility for the conservation of the physical and human resources of the nation.

2. As the service "at the front" is now recognized to involve routine drudgery and irksome duties with little of the glory or excitement formerly associated with military life, so it must be remembered that the duties of the women may be in large measure humble and laborious, but must be performed in a spirit of loyal and patient service and in that spirit only will they bring their reward.

3. These tasks will not necessitate the neglect of more important duties and obligations.

4. The type of tasks has in view the fitness of women whose training has been primarily that of students preparing in general for teaching or domestic life.

5. The tasks offered are of different grades of severity and of capacity for expansion.

6. The tasks are varied in character to correspond with the different aptitudes of students.

7. The tasks are in general such as may be performed without interference with duties already assumed.

8. The tasks are such that the students may continue them on leaving the University and on taking up work in other communities.

9. The services which may be rendered are of value in times of peace as well as in times of war.

These principles were presented in printed form and there followed the "Pledge" and program of activities:

PLEDGE

Realizing that my country needs the loyal service of all its women, both now and in time of peace, I pledge myself to the tasks I have indicated, by checking individual items, on this sheet; and I will undertake to perform these duties as conscientiously as if I were formally enlisted for military service.

1. I agree to make an effort to increase my physical strength and vigor.

2. I agree to help some young person to increase his physical strength and vigor.

3. I agree to wear a costume adapted to my occupation, avoiding waste and display.

4. I agree to promote economy in food supplies by (a) the observance of rational economy in my personal use of food; (b) organizing groups of women for the study of food economy.

5. I agree to foster the proper use of foods by learning how to prepare them.

6. I agree to aid in increasing the food supply by (a) personally cultivating a plot of land; (b) helping to organize groups of children to plant gardens in unoccupied lots.

7. I agree to take an active part in some organized movement for the prevention of infant mortality.

8. I agree to take an active part in a child-welfare agency.

9. I agree to inform myself as to approved methods of school nursing and to do all in my power to introduce this means of conserving the health of children in the schools of my community.

10. I agree to help provide for the children and dependent members of the family of a man or woman "at the front" in war or industry.

11. I agree, realizing that vice and alcoholism in increasing measure accompany war, and believing that future generations should be given by birth the best in health and mind that ethical living among men can bestow, to urge that marriage should take place only among those who can show that they are free from any disease which may be transmitted to future generations.

12. I agree to establish friendly relations with persons whose families came to this country more recently than mine, and in this and every possible way to help promote a feeling of international sympathy.

13. I agree to study the various proposals which have been brought forward for the establishment of a Society of Nations and organized common peace and to do all in my power to build a new social order based, not on mutual distrust and selfish competition, but on confidence and good will, upon the spirit of service and cooperation.

14. I agree, provided my scholarship and health are adequate, to register for one of the following courses, each to count as a half-major, and taken without fee:

I. "Social Service in War Time."
II. "Food: Conservation and Production."
III. "First Aid."

I elaborated many of these suggestions and explained their significance. I urged the students to use their influence to support all agencies for social welfare which had had a serious setback in other nations and to see to it that children be kept in school and the child labor laws not be broken down under the guise of the country's needs. I pointed out that it was for the old to counsel and for the young to act, and told how impressed we were with the power and influence young women represented in the national crisis; and I ended by congratulating them on their opportunity to conserve the nation in the noblest sense.

The meeting closed with the singing of "America." It was a very solemn procession that wended its way to classrooms, libraries, and laboratories. Almost immediately requests came pouring in from colleges and high schools for copies of our program, and then letters telling with gratitude of the help we had given.

Arrangements were made for the immediate registration of students in the new courses. In spite of programs of study which were already heavy, 86 registered for "Social Service in War Time," 30 for "Conservation and Production of Food," and 130 for "First Aid." A branch of the Red Cross was established at the University and made use of the interest of the students in promoting its special activities. The making of war supplies under careful supervision, active service at infant welfare stations, weekly meetings for the study of the prevention of infant mortality and the promotion of child welfare, and weekly addresses describing various ways by which college women could aid in preserving and promoting right conditions in education, health, labor, and international relations during war were other activities in which the women students took part.

It was natural that the normal social life of the students should break down. The number of men students fell off, and the majority of those who remained in the University were drafted into the Students Officers' Training Corps and put under military discipline. It was not strange or unanticipated that some of the measures adopted were futile and wasteful. A rather amusing instance occurred when Lexington Hall was taken over for use as a mess hall. Early in the morning the whole Corps was marched to the Hall for breakfast with military precision; but, as only one section at a time could be accommodated, ranks were broken and the hungry left-overs, many of them chafing to be about their business, made themselves as comfortable as they could sitting on the curbstone until they could enter the Hall, when the breakfasted group would take their places on the curb. Then, when all had been fed, all marched away. But sitting on the curb gave no occupation except to stare up at Beecher Hall. As this was the time of day when the women students were rising, they had to do some gymnastics to roll out of bed, creep along the floor in their night clothes, and do some sleight of hand to get the windows closed without being seen by the United States Army. My suggestion to the commanding officer that, if it was not practicable to assign those who had breakfasted to other tasks, they might be required to sit on the opposite curb with their backs to Beecher Hall was received courteously and the necessary orders issued. In consequence it was no longer necessary to keep up the "daily-dozen" habit.

It is commonly believed that a military uniform has a special attraction for women regardless of who occupies it, but there was no evidence of this at the University. The women simply went about their business and paid no attention to members of the Corps either as individuals or as companies.

The University was almost immediately brought face to face with a difficult problem. Organizations and individuals seeking the help of large numbers of women in carrying on their various activities turned to the University as a source from which, without much trouble to themselves, they could secure promptly the services of intelligent and efficient young women. Appeals came in in rapid succession. Now it was for one hundred "girls"—a word taboo in the University—to dance the following evening at the Soldiers and Sailors Club; then it was for ninety women to take the place of men in the Ordnance Division of the War Department; or for fifty women to go to the railroad station to meet and welcome incoming troops; or for a group to organize for the conservation of platinum (women who practically never saw even gold!). It was necessary to formulate a general policy. This was done speedily by the older women. We decided first that under no circumstances would we encourage women students to undertake outside activities which would interfere either with their health or with duties to which they were already pledged; and second, that the University would not place the students under official compulsion to participate in any of the undertakings proposed. We made these requests known, and left the decision to the students and their parents. If, for instance, we were asked to provide Sunday dinner and entertainment in private families, we would reply that the University could not interfere with family arrangements. We felt the less loath to take this position when we learned how bored or self-conscious the men often were on finding themselves in unwonted social surroundings and how they often greatly preferred some free time to use as they felt inclined. We organized, however, a series of social affairs at Ida Noyes Hall and sent word to Fort Sheridan and the Naval Training Station that men would be welcome at certain times. Even for this service we were careful not to make a general appeal to the women. We selected a considerable number whose social experience and understanding and whose good judgment and well-bred manners we could trust, and then gave them the option of helping in carrying out the plan. In every case they were friendly and courteous, and we never saw a case of forwardness or laxity of conduct. We had ample evidence that the students were giving their co-operation in social affairs in the city quite generously; but it was always on an individual or family, not official, basis.

During the summer it became evident to the university as a whole that much work which had been undertaken by various committees was overlapping, and a scheme was proposed to President Judson whereby a series of committees was organized to make efficient use of all types of service which members of the University could render. Miss Elizabeth Wallace was made chairman of the Committee on Women Student Activities, and she thereupon organized the Woman Students' Training Corps, whose members signed the following pledge:

As a member of the Woman Students' Training Corps I promise:

1. That while in college I will prepare myself for some essential occupation whereby I may serve my country efficiently in my own home or elsewhere.

2. That after leaving college, and during the major portion of long vacations, I will practice an essential occupation for the duration of the war.

3. Furthermore, I pledge myself to support the President of the United States, to honor the flag, and to uphold by my acts and influence the best ideals of American womanhood.

As a loyal member of the University of Chicago, I hereby pledge my faith.

Date: ....

Signature: ....

This Corps engaged in different activities, but one of its best results was the discovery and development of individual gifts of leadership. Later it was reorganized and became the Federation of University Women.

Shortly after the close of the war it gratified me intensely to make known to the women students the following letter from the Acting President of the University:

CHICAGO, DECEMBER 16, 1918

MY DEAR MISS TALBOT:

I do not know that any proper occasion will present itself to say to the women of the University what I should nevertheless like in some manner to convey to them, namely, my warm appreciation of the remarkably fine way in which they have carried themselves throughout the past quarter. The conditions have been in many particulars exasperating, and such as to interfere seriously with the legitimate work of the institution. I have yet to hear of any serious complaint, however. The women seem to have accepted the situation in a wholly fine spirit, to have subordinated themselves as far as possible to the exigencies of the military situation, and to have made themselves useful in a great variety of ways.

I trust the coming quarter will see a restoration of our normal equilibrium, and of the opportunities which the women of the University have heretofore enjoyed.

Yours very truly,

[*Signed*] *James R. Angell*

It must be admitted, however, that this admirable record was followed by a reaction similar in nature to that which took place in every one of the warring countries and which astonished and shocked the world. The period of self-control bore fruit, however, and no such general breakdown in decent standards of social life was evident at the University as was common in other large cities the world around.

Shortly after the close of the war, an incident occurred which was of interest in its implications. The La Verne Noyes Foundation, valued at a million and a half dollars, was established July 5, 1918, by the munificent gift of Mr. La Verne Noyes. It provides tuition fees for students who (1) shall themselves have served in the Army or Navy of the United States in the war for liberty into which the Republic entered on April 6, 1917, providing that such service was terminated by honorable discharge; or (2) shall be descendants by blood of anyone in service in the Army or Navy of the United States who served in said war; or (3) shall be descendants by blood of anyone who served in the Army or Navy of the United States in said war, provided that such service was terminated by an honorable death or an honorable discharge. The first public instructions in regard to the filing of applications were characterized by the use of masculine terms: "men," "he," "his," etc. I straightway wrote to the Dean in charge of the fund, asking if women would be eligible. He replied in his characteristically blunt way, "No," with the idea "how absurd" permeating the seeming ultimatum. I then inquired directly of the War and Navy departments as to whether women had served in the war in the Army or Navy, and was informed officially that they had served in both. Before these replies came, I kept the question open by correspondence with the Dean and other authorities, feeling perhaps unduly confident that I was showing more moderation in my phrases than was my correspondent. The matter was closed to my satisfaction by an official administrative ruling that there would be no distinction of sex either in progenitor or scion, though I think these are not the exact terms used in the statement which is officially on file.

Epilogue

The building of a university is an unending process unless by unhappy chance mental decrepitude, educational arrogance, or dulness of vision beset its builders. These brief reminiscences reveal a few, perhaps rather slight, phases of the building of the University of Chicago. The years which have passed since this record closed have shown that the process has not slackened. From the beginning its builders have realized fully the words of President Warren of Boston University that "that educational institution is poor indeed that has no wants"—wants ranging from endowments to laboratories, libraries to administrative facilities, scholarly teachers to men and women gifted in research and above all devoted to truth. It is a commonplace to say that what has been accomplished at Chicago is a marvel. From what was in 1892 a rather forlorn bit of prairie there have gone to the furthermost parts of the earth men and women who have been nurtured by the University and who are eager to carry its spirit. The old nickname of "Harper's Bazaar," conceived in ridicule, has given place to world-wide esteem. It has been a wonderful experience for me to watch what has happened and to have had some share in it; but of all the memories I have connected with it, there is none more vivid than that of the unfailing, generous, and sympathetic co-operation given me by faculty, officers, and students, both men and women alike. There is hardly a flaw in the record. The load I carried was an absorbing one. For thirty-three years I gave all I had to the University, and reaped a rich

Marion Talbot, 1925

harvest of happiness and content. So it happened that on my retirement when a well-meaning but not very successful dean of women said, "I congratulate you.—Now you can do what you want to do," I flared back, "That is what I have been doing all these years—if it had not seemed the most worth while thing I could do, I would have dropped it instantly." A rather recent graduate told me she had intended to be a dean of women but had decided there was too much drudgery about it. "Drudgery," I replied, "how can there be drudgery when you are just trying to help human beings!"

So it was not strange that after my retirement in 1925 I took satisfaction in two terms of service as acting-president of Constantinople Woman's College. There, too, were the opportunities to help solve difficult problems and to give sympathy and encouragement. There, too, I met much of the friendly spirit of the University, which was one of its most precious assets. There, too, as through all the years, I found constant stimulus in the motto of the University:

Crescat scientia, vita excolatur